BLOCKCHAIN AND THE DIGITAL ECONOMY

BLOCKCHAIN AND THE DIGITAL ECONOMY

The socio-economic impact of blockchain technology

Fred Steinmetz, Lennart Ante
and Ingo Fiedler

agenda
publishing

First published in 2020 by Agenda Publishing

Agenda Publishing Limited
The Core
Bath Lane
Newcastle Helix
Newcastle upon Tyne
NE4 5TF
www.agendapub.com

ISBN 978-1-78821-224-3 (hardcover)
ISBN 978-1-78821-225-0 (paperback)

Blockchain Research Lab

British Library Cataloguing-in-Publication Data
A catalogue record for this book is available from the British Library

Typeset by Newgen Publishing UK
Printed and bound in the UK by TJ International

Contents

Contents

Preface

A decade has passed since Bitcoin's invention. Bitcoin and its underlying blockchain technology, so the promise goes, is poised to do for value what the internet has for information. The internet has enabled the easy and immediate transfer of practically all and any information. Blockchain technology has the potential to make a variety of processes much more efficient by enabling the transmission of value by a protocol without the need for expensive intermediaries. But is the mere potential enough to make the bold claims around the blockchain hype realistic? What has actually evolved during the last ten years and what is likely to happen in the next decade?

The aim of this book is to demystify blockchain and its surrounding hype. We give readers a basic knowledge of the technology involved and explain its different aspects so that its potential and implications can be fully appreciated, and the reader can make their own differentiated assessment of when the use of blockchain technology makes sense and when it does not. Our aim is to provide a balanced overview of the current status of blockchain. However, how society will embrace or reject the various options that blockchain technology offers is still unclear. A grounded discussion of its socio-economic implications has to include some speculation of future developments. We engage in some of this speculation but also explain real examples of blockchain implementations, which we hope enables the reader to distinguish between actual applications, realistic potentials and mere fantasies.

Centralization constitutes an integral paradigm in modern societies. Most of the services that we interact with – even interaction between individuals – is enabled and processed by some kind of intermediary.

Whether this is Facebook for communicating with friends, Google for finding information on the internet or a commercial bank for taking out a loan. Centralized architectures ensure the control and efficient management of a service provider over the access to a service. This is, however, the perspective of the service provider. The centralization of interactions through intermediation makes us dependent on them and we have to trust that they will do what we ask for. Moreover, these structures inherently produce costs and other disadvantages for the individual. These costs can be the personal data that has been voluntarily submitted to Facebook's servers, which is (almost) freely utilized and monetized. Costs can simply be a straightforward fee that an intermediary might charge a company for referring a customer to conduct a purchase. Of course, this fee can be incorporated into the product's price and passed on to the customer. There is no question that such services provide additional value to customers, whether they have optimized the search of desired offerings, provided a social communication platform or facilitated monetary transactions. There is, however, the implication that there is a cost of centralization levied by the intermediary in one way or another. Faced by a lack of alternatives for certain services (such as banking), customers and society in general accept and pay these costs.

A prominent example of costs for individual users of Facebook is the data leak of 2018, in which central servers of the company were hacked. Centralized systems are prone to cyber-attacks, because they present single points of failure. Once a centralized database or entity has been compromised, all data is disclosed to the attacker. On social and economic levels, this has enormous ramifications, as social interaction and economic trade rely on technical infrastructures that are most often centralized. The result is dependency on the intermediary to protect its users' data and an extensive requirement for trust by the individual using the system. As social life and economic interaction is increasingly organized and conducted digitally, these dependencies become more important. The paradigm of decentralization promises to reduce these dependencies on third parties – responsibility, authority and control are distributed across users.

While at first glance blockchain seems to be a complex issue with many facets, it is actually nothing more than a clever combination of different technical and economic aspects of existing decentralized applications that are embodied in code. It can be regarded as the logical descendant of peer-to-peer (P2P) networks, but with far reaching potential. Blockchain assembles existing technologies and mechanisms to distribute tasks currently conducted by selected intermediaries onto the shoulders of many processors. These processors are not altruistic benefactors but are compensated for their efforts while acting as a control instance on each other. In a blockchain system, interaction is facilitated directly through technical P2P connections. As with Bitcoin, the first and high-profile implementation of a blockchain in 2009, transactions of a digital asset are transferred directly between two peers. The scope for blockchain, however, reaches well beyond cryptocurrencies. Numerous other applications for the technology are envisioned and currently being developed. These include, for example, digital money, which is comparable to cash and issued by central banks; improved energy markets in which energy can be traded efficiently in microgrids; transparent and efficient capital markets, which allow non-accredited investors to profit from the economic success of companies; traceable supply chains which allow consumers to verify a product's origins; a transparent and verifiably fair gambling industry; and the empowerment of individuals over their own personal data. Blockchain technology can also facilitate an infrastructure for efficiently valuing, renting or selling access to personal data. Such data marketplaces imply individuals' autonomous control over their digitized personal data and, to return to the Facebook example above, make the requesters and collectors of such data pay for its usage. As a consequence, personal data is valued via a market price and the data used to personalize offerings or train algorithms is of a higher quality compared to those collected today.

Regardless of the challenges, limitations and shortcomings blockchain technology currently faces, the vast increase in attention from media, corporations and academia towards the technology reflects its increasing relevance for society. However, the implications of this potential new technological paradigm have not yet reached a broader public debate, nor have economic and societal implications been sufficiently addressed by academia. This is where our motivation for investigating the technology and writing this book stems from and why we founded the Blockchain Research Lab. Our aim is, on the one hand, to further the general understanding of the blockchain technology and, on the other hand, to analyze the resulting challenges and opportunities and their socio-economic consequences. The discussions in this book involve some speculation about societal changes in the future. These are based on the best of our knowledge and necessarily involve subjective elements. As optimists and believers in decentralized technologies we do envisage and describe the societal risks of adopting such technologies but are convinced that the positives can outweigh the negatives. Our discussions on the potential and actual socio-economic impacts reflect this view.

This book is divided into four main parts. Readers are first introduced to the technology itself, in Chapter 1, and given an initial superficial impression of what the technology is about and its potential uses. Chapter 2 offers a more detailed overview of the technical components that make up blockchain: P2P technology, mathematical and cryptographic elements, such as hash algorithms, but also economic and social components, such as consensus building, governance and incentive mechanisms. Chapter 3 deals with the socio-economic effects of decentralization, including information about the ownership and adaptation of cryptocurrencies, censorship resistance and how blockchain enables the creation of entirely new markets. Finally, in Chapter 4, particular cases of application are described. This includes the disruption of existing markets, the development of completely new markets or visions for markets which have yet to be foreseen in the near future, for example, local peer-to-peer energy markets.

Figures and tables

FIGURES

Figures and tables

TABLES

Introducing blockchain

To appreciate the potential that blockchain technology offers, we need to explain how blockchain systems work and what their key characteristics are. We aim to keep the description simple and accessible and work our way through the various elements that make up the blockchain system step by step.

In its pure form, blockchain can be described as a data structure or database. In a broader sense, blockchain is a decentralized system or network that combines certain technologies to create an exchange environment for its participants (Kosba *et al.* 2016; Bonneau *et al.* 2016). More specifically, blockchain is a highly sophisticated construct of intersecting and interconnected elements of technology and economic incentivization. The overarching goal of such constructs is to create a trusted setting for participants of equal status to facilitate frictionless and un-intermediated interaction, exchange or messaging. The motivation for decentralizing the infrastructure of social and economic interaction comes from decreasing trust towards profit-driven, vulnerable or potentially corrupt third parties, while enhancing the security and efficiency of such interactions. The solution design emphasizes an open (accessible) network of participants (peers), whose interests are aligned through economic incentives and the responsibilities and duties of centralized authorities are distributed across many different parties. At the same time, such systems are fault-tolerant against manipulative and fraudulent behaviour.

Fundamental to blockchain networks is the concept of a shared ledger, which constitutes the verifiably one and only database of all state changes between all participants. The idea of a transparent shared ledger enables all participants to verify which transactions have been processed in the past and led to the current state of distribution. This high level of transparency is necessary for distributing the coordination tasks, formerly performed by intermediaries, onto the shoulders of many. In contrast to siloed and inaccessible databases that are separately maintained by each participant, a shared ledger reduces the need for costly database reconciliations. Instead, agreeing on the current state of a database in a blockchain network is designed as a collaborative process by all participants based on consensus mechanisms. A key innovation of blockchain technology is the scalability of such consensus mechanisms, which means that a potentially unlimited number of participants can become part of a blockchain network without decelerating its functionality. The shared ledger is the outcome of a chronological and continuous search for consensus about past and current states of distribution.

The shared ledger, commonly referred to as "distributed ledger" or blockchain, has been recognized to facilitate a change in how ownership is regarded and managed in a digitized world. While in centralized systems, ownership, for example, of a land title is assigned by a single institution and based on a central database, ownership in a blockchain system is the result of distributed verification procedures and manifested in a non-corruptible database. Ownership in this instance can refer to personal data, digitized shares or real-world assets like houses. This basically means that the exchange of information itself or simply access to information can be exchanged, as well as (the ownership of) digital representations of physical objects. Blockchain presents the technical infrastructure for ensuring such exchanges' integrity without involving a trusted middleman. More on the concept of ledgers, their meanings for society and their evolution is provided at the beginning of Chapter 3.

1.1 A TRANSACTION

In the following, we will walk through the steps taken in a transfer in a generalized model of a blockchain. Figure 1.1 shows the highlighted steps. A transaction request undergoes certain validation processes

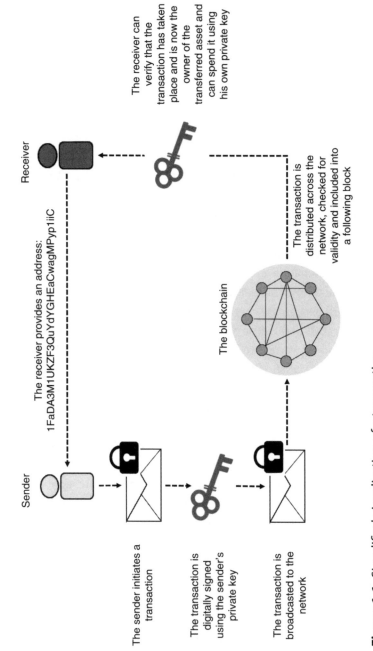

Figure 1.1 Simplified visualization of a transaction

Source: adapted from Tepper (2015).

The receiver can verify that the transaction has taken place and is now the owner of the transferred asset and can spend it using his own private key

Receiver

The receiver provides an address: 1FaDA3M1UKZF3QuYdYGHEaCwagMPyp1iiC

Sender

The transaction is distributed across the network, checked for validity and included into a following block

The blockchain

The sender initiates a transaction

The transaction is digitally signed using the sender's private key

The transaction is broadcasted to the network

and, if these processes are successful, end up in a state change including the transaction. Following the state change, the transacted asset can be transferred again. So far this also describes a transaction in a traditional centralized system. The overarching goal of both centralized and decentralized systems is to verify the validity of a transaction request, confirming that the sender is the owner of the subject to be transferred and thus has the right to transfer it, and consequently to manifest valid transfers into a generally accepted state of distribution.

In a blockchain system, however, the initial transaction request is not directed to a third party but towards a network of participants, who verify the authenticity and validity of the transfer. The technical connections in the network of all participants are the foundation of the system and facilitate the direct transfer between sender and receiver. These networks are referred to as P2P networks, which themselves are an important innovation in the evolution of the internet and a crucial technical foundation of blockchain systems.

The network participants are incentivized to verify the validity of the transfer request. If a network participant receives the transfer request, it is verified and forwarded to other connected peers, only if the verification has been successful. If a transfer request is not valid for whatever reason, it is not forwarded. This presents a first barrier for manipulative attacks against the network through false transaction propagation. In the best case, a transfer request is forwarded across the whole network, so every peer verifies the transfer request. The processes of verification are enabled through applied cryptography – another crucial component of blockchain technology. Cryptographic means are applied for anonymization purposes and data compression. Cryptography allows the creation of verifiable signatures, enabling the network to point transactions to sender and receiver. Following this, an initiator of a transaction is verified as the actual sender through a digital signature.

Within the network, the transaction is one of many. At pre-defined intervals, newly verified transactions are assembled into bulks. These bulks are the main body of blocks which form a container for verified transactions adding metadata, for example, timestamps and cryptographic references to previous blocks, to the assembly of transactions.

A block itself presents a data package, which is also propagated across the network. Just like the transaction, a block's validity can be easily verified by other network participants. The structure of the block allows the network to continuously add bulks of transactions to the existing database – the blockchain. The blockchain is the chronological chain of cryptographically connected blocks and presents the foundational database of all state changes ever conducted in the network.

Instead of continuously adding new verified transactions to a transaction chain, the block structure introduces a bulk-wise state change, on which the whole network agrees upon. An important function of blocks is to create certainty about the chronological order of transactions. If transactions were added to a transaction chain, it would be more complicated for network participants to clarify which transaction, of two or more conflicting transactions, occurred first. Moreover, the block structure allows relevant data in the network to be compressed – the compression of data allows "lightweight" nodes to be created, which do not need to carry the full load of a blockchain, but still are able to verify the validity of blocks and inherent transactions.

Because the verification processes and the formation of blocks are computationally costly, incentivization schemes ensure that participants are motivated to take part in the verification tasks and are compensated accordingly. The most prominent algorithm to ground the incentivization of such activity is the proof-of-work (PoW) applied in Bitcoin. It basically creates a competitive task for all validators to find a validity parameter for a new block. This parameter needs to be found in a repetitive process and can only be solved through trial and error. More computational power relative to the network increases the chances of finding the parameter. The parameter itself serves as a verifier for other network participants, which means it is very hard to generate but easy to verify. Most importantly, generating the desired parameter justifies the validator's creation of a transaction of their own that includes a block formation reward. Moreover, the successful validator receives transaction fees that are incorporated in transactions by the initiators and increase the probability of a transaction being included in the next block and thus of having the transfer validated. Other mechanisms employ different approaches to incentivize participants to verify and validate transactions. There are numerous mechanisms for network participants to decide on who adds blocks to the chain – referred to as finding consensus. The consensus mechanisms are another important element of blockchain technology. They are interrelated with the governance of a system and its incentivization patterns.

For the transaction request in question, this means that it undergoes verification procedures and is eventually propagated across all nodes in the network. In the course of the consensus mechanism, the transaction request is included in one of the following blocks, and this block extends the blockchain. The most recent block of the blockchain represents the current state of distribution, which means that the transaction is final, and the transferred asset has a new owner.

1.2 KEY CHARACTERISTICS

Blockchain's innovation is to combine existing technologies in a sophisticated and beneficial manner. A core feature of the technology for public blockchain systems is not that a network of participants decides who conducts the processes previously conducted by a central party, but that the network functions despite consisting of participants who are completely unknown to one another – they have no reputation and are not required to disclose their identity. Regardless of the constellation of participants in the network, even if it consists of unknown actors, the design of blockchains with their technical, mathematical as well as economic and political components allows a sender to trust in the functionality of the system rather than in the people operating it.

A core characteristic of these systems is that they operate without the need for trust between parties. The trust-free environment of blockchain networks is facilitated through their transparent data structure and processing and the implementation of economic incentives, which safeguard the alignment of interests of the majority of network nodes. The necessity for participants to trust a third party to adequately process the respective transaction is not diminished, but the participants' trust is mitigated by open-source, freely accessible and verifiable software. Trust is shifted from human interaction to computer code, from a small number of authorities, or even a single one, to multiple verifiably incentivized validators and from hidden to transparent processes. Bitcoin is the best example of a functional public blockchain system that contrasts existing incumbent and centralized structures, concepts of ownership and fiscal control. Bitcoin was invented shortly after and seemingly inspired by the financial crisis in 2007/08, when the established financial system disclosed its vulnerabilities and trust in governments and financial institutions declined. Such dichotomy certainly presents a major driver for Bitcoin's attractiveness.

Most transaction systems today are centralized in their design: a central party confirms, conducts and settles transactions. Inherent to conventional centralized transaction systems is the necessity for the validation of transaction data through a central trusted party, which results in processing costs and performance bottlenecks at central servers. In contrast, a transaction in the blockchain network can be conducted between any two individuals without the authentication of such a central party. Transactions in a blockchain system are processed and validated by the interplay of all network nodes, which participate in the consensus mechanism – the system is thus decentralized. Decentralization can have many meanings and levels, which we will address in the course of this book. As all transaction data is continuously replicated across all nodes, the need for an intermediary to share and maintain the ledger is eliminated. In this manner, blockchain can significantly reduce the server costs, including the development cost and the operational costs of the processing tasks and thus mitigate the performance bottlenecks of the central server architecture (Zheng *et al.* 2018).

The distribution of processing tasks to many participants inherently requires the system to provide a certain level of transparency. For validators to reach consensus on updates of the blockchain, they need to be able to control each other. State changes following transactions in the network are therefore publicly visible and timestamped, thereby creating a chain of ownership changes. The distributed and transparent

7

nature of blockchain allows any transaction event to be traced. Each update in the state of an asset can be traced back to its origin as each block is linked to the previous block by cryptography. An attacker attempting to manipulate a specific block in the blockchain would need to recalculate all subsequent blocks. Practically, making such attacks is infeasible, because they need the attacker to provide tremendous capacities of computing power and convince the majority of the network that their version of the blockchain is true. Thus, the blockchain can be regarded as immutable, if certain levels of transparency are provided in the respective blockchain system and sufficient computing power is dedicated to securing the network.

Moreover, public blockchain systems are accessible to anyone with a device and an internet connection. The basic software setup is a wallet software. Often the code foundations of blockchain projects are open-source. This enables anyone to review the code and verify how it works. The transparency of code improves users' understanding and trust towards the functionality of such systems. Furthermore, the transparency of the code fosters innovation in the blockchain space as it allows anyone to contribute to existing code or copy and improve it.

In the realm of the accessibility of public blockchain systems, the consensus algorithm is of special interest, because finding consensus is a complex procedure in distributed systems. It is not always the case that a distributed system is capable of handling an increasing number of users. This is referred to as the scalability of a consensus algorithm – the capability of a distributed system to retain its functionality with an increasing number of users. The consensus algorithm applied in Bitcoin's system is highly scalable and capable of a massive increase in users. In fact, user increase can also increase the connections among peers in the network. The system's functionality remains unaffected, and the more users are engaged in the consensus mechanism, the more secure the system becomes as the computational power dedicated to the network increases. Greater interconnectivity among peers further improves the processes of transaction and block propagation. The term scalability is also used in the context of the technical capability of a blockchain system for validating transactions. For payment-focused blockchain systems to compete with centralized payment solutions such as Visa and Mastercard, a commonly cited threshold of 10,000 transactions per second must be achievable. With regard to Bitcoin, the most widely distributed cryptocurrency, the blockchain can currently process up to 7 transactions per second (Zheng *et al.* 2018), as a block formation interval is set to 10 minutes on average and block sizes for transaction data are limited. However, numerous projects address the topic of scalability using different technical approaches, such as the Lightning Network, which is effectively an additional layer over the Bitcoin network.

Other than in public blockchain systems, specialized blockchain systems exist in which participants are known identities and are of limited numbers. Running a system of known identities eliminates the necessity for employing complex algorithms and thus allows to increase the transaction throughput within the system. Such systems are referred to as "private" or "permissioned" blockchains. Public and private blockchain systems can be differentiated by the accessibility of using the system – whether a user can become a part of the network by its own or someone else's decision (*private* versus *public*). Furthermore, they can be differentiated by the ability of a user to participate in the validation of transactions – whether a user can decide on its own to become a validator or someone else decides (*permissionless* versus *permissioned*). In the course of this book, the blockchain model which is being referred to in the explicit context is always clarified.

During the evolution of blockchain systems and designs, some blockchain projects have emerged which facilitate a special functionality. These additional technical components are called "virtual machines" and allow complex computations to be executed within the blockchain environment. Other than in Bitcoin, platforms such as Ethereum allow users to upload computational code onto the blockchain using specific transaction types. This permits users to program transactions to be executed on the occurrence of pre-defined events. These programs are referred to as smart contracts, which add further characteristics to certain blockchain systems: automation and autonomy. The complexity of the code to be executed is literally unlimited, which creates further potential uses for the technology. All kinds of interactions can potentially be executed autonomously and automatically.

1.3 CATEGORIES

Since the invention of Bitcoin, a decade ago, the concept of blockchain has developed in diverse ways. While Bitcoin and most blockchains that followed are publicly accessible, in the sense that everyone can participate and use the network, the concept of blockchain has also been adapted for use in private, mostly business-focused, settings. The motivation for creating private blockchain systems lies in reducing infrastructure costs of interactions between participants, improved coordination among participants and increased transparency of interaction. Access to private blockchain systems is restricted to an exclusive circle of companies/entities, which, for example, might track a certain product along its supply chain and life cycle. Accordingly, different models of blockchains can be differentiated among their level of technical decentralization. While public blockchains are tendentially decentralized because they are scalable in terms of increasing numbers of users, private blockchain systems are often tendentially centralized, because a limited number of participants can increase the performance and control of a blockchain system. In private blockchain systems the participants are often identified companies and it is not in the interest of private blockchain participants to transparently reveal transactional data to the public – access to the respective blockchain data is therefore restricted. In sum, two dimensions are required for differentiating blockchain systems: (1) the accessibility for use and participation and (2) the accessibility of transaction data.

Garzik (2015) differentiates the access to transaction data as either public or private. The access to use and to participate in the network, for example through transaction-processing, can either be permissioned or "permissionless" (Table 1.1). The most prominent combination is the public and permissionless blockchain network Bitcoin. Numerous other

Table 1.1 Categories of blockchains based on access to transaction-processing and access to data

Access to transactions	*Access to transaction-processing*	
	Permissioned	*Permissionless*
Public	Proprietary coloured coins protocols	Existing cryptocurrencies (Bitcoin, Ethereum, ...)
Private	Access limited to pre-selected transaction-processors	Not applicable

Source: adapted from Garzik (2015).

blockchain systems are in existence, each competing for users and developers to join their network for increasing their system's relative and absolute relevance. Some public blockchain projects are pursuing the goal of providing a high throughput of transactions, which led them to restrict the access to transaction-processing to a limited number of known and reputable companies/entities, which users can elect. Private blockchains are conceptualized in a similar way. Transaction-processing is often outsourced to service providers, restricted to reputable companies or allocated randomly to participants who also act as validators. The limitation of transaction processors thereby facilitates the implementation of less complex consensus algorithms, which improves performance capabilities. However, some experts argue that the complexity of public blockchains' consensus algorithms is a crucial invention which secures the immutability of the transaction data. In the course of this book, we will explain both the functionality of public blockchains' consensus and its innovative character (Chapter 2) as well as blockchain applications which do not necessarily require such complexity (Chapter 4).

For some types of applications, some characteristics of public blockchains are incompatible and insufficient for their purposes. This can relate to the level of transparency of transaction data, which can be disclosed to competitors or contain sensitive information, or a limited transaction throughput. Such applications can be in energy markets, in which blockchains are applied as coordinative tools, or digital identity schemes, in which a user can selectively grant access to personal information. In the latter example, the blockchain can record and coordinate claims and serves as the technical base for a digital rights management system. We will dig deeper in the topic of digital identity management using blockchain infrastructure during Chapter 3 and in particular in Chapter 4 on self-sovereign identity.

The term "distributed ledger technology" (DLT) is often used interchangeably with blockchain technology. The term "blockchain" originates from Satoshi Nakamoto's whitepaper about Bitcoin, in which he describes the chaining of blocks. In the realm of other cryptocurrencies, whose databases are often closely related to Bitcoin's blockchain, and which share the characteristic of public accessibility, the term blockchain prevails. DLT describes a broader set of variants which pursue the same goals of a blockchain but vary in technical aspects. The term also includes categories of private and permissioned system types and blockchain can be considered a category of DLT. Moreover, DLT comprises those system types that have native assets as well as those that do not.

As indicated above, blockchain systems can be differentiated with reference to the implementation of blockchain-native assets. As we will explain in Chapter 4, there are numerous applications of blockchain technology, which do not require a coin or token, whose transactions are tracked by the blockchain and whose value can be volatile (as in the case of Bitcoin). These blockchain-native assets are in existence to incentivize transaction-processing, but they can have different functionalities other than digital cash. In contrast, private blockchain systems are usually limited to a number of known participants, whose profits for maintaining a blockchain are efficiency gains from the collaborative and transparent processing of business- or product-related information within their system – they do not require a native asset.

While a coin represents a native asset of a blockchain on the infrastructure level, we define a token as a coin which is created by a smart contract. As smart contracts and tokens are tied to underlying blockchains, they circulate on the blockchain that carries the code of the smart contract (the infrastructure). They can be transferred like a coin among peers but using transactions on the underlying blockchain. This way, tokens can be easily created while inheriting the security and functionality of the underlying blockchain. The most prominent example is Ethereum, whose coin is Ether but which allows for easily creating other tokens through smart contracts.

The concept of tokenization is quite powerful as it diminishes the need to create a single blockchain for every project which plans to create a coin and can increase the use and relevance of the underlying blockchain system. The concept of tokenization is also powerful in the sense that they can represent digital assets, or digital replicas of physical assets. This way, previously intangible assets, such as voting rights, can be tokenized. Tokenizing voting rights allows for experimentation with the concept of liquid democracy, in which voters have the right to assign (transfer) their voting right to someone who they think is capable of making a better, more informed decision. The ease of transferring tokens is also suitable for digitized shares, which a shareholder could hold in their personal wallet and sell instantly on a dedicated market. The potential social impact that the tokenizing of existing assets, new assets or access rights can have will be highlighted in Chapter 3 in which we elaborate on blockchain's potential to facilitate the creation of new markets and marketplaces, and in Chapter 4 in which we describe blockchain applications in capital markets.

Blockchain technology comprises models with different levels of decentralization and accessibility by design. As such, it forms a continuum of system designs, rather than a uniform solution. Technically, there are numerous levels of restricting access to both the transparency of records, for example through encryption, and the processing of transactions, for example through setting up certain financial requirements for validators. In combination with native assets, the complexity of differentiation increases, because such assets may have functionalities that are inaccessible to certain types of users, or there may even be multiple native assets. With respect to the use of the term "decentralization", it is used extensively in the context of blockchain technology, mostly as a positive and key characteristic of blockchains, and therefore a superior concept in general. However, depending on the context, decentralization has different meanings, such as for political theory, computer science or in the context of blockchain networks (Schneider 2019). In the course of this book, we will refer to different aspects of decentralization, including the technical decentralization (peer-to-peer networks) and the political decentralization in blockchain's governance models both in Chapter 2, and with respect to blockchain's socio-economic impacts in Chapter 3.

Now that we have outlined the basic ideas behind blockchain, in the following chapter we will delve into how the technical, mathematical as well as economic and political components are combined in blockchain systems. The detailed description of these components is necessary for a comprehensive understanding of how these systems function, their implications for society and how they can be applied. The constructs of blockchains are complex but understanding its basic components and how they are assembled lays the foundation for understanding the uses that follow. We also explore why people use and trust such systems, a topic which we will investigate more fully in Chapter 3 on cryptocurrency usage, knowledge and motivations by presenting the results of research conducted by the Blockchain Research Lab among German internet users.

2

Blockchain's basic components

The best way to explain blockchain is to break it down into its basic components. We define components as the applied technologies and concepts which are either standalone technologies or concepts in computer science, which have been researched for decades in contexts other than blockchain. We identify technical and mathematical components as well as economic, political and social concepts, which are intertwined to facilitate blockchains' functionalities. The aim of this chapter is to provide an overview of the applied technologies and concepts and an understanding of how they are combined.

First, we will explain the technical components, including P2P networks, virtual machines and smart contracts. Depending on the perspective, many blockchain systems can indeed be categorized as specific types of P2P systems, because P2P technology is the technical foundation of blockchain systems whose purpose is the exchange of verifiably unique assets. Whether P2P systems are considered forerunners of blockchain systems or a component of blockchain systems, understanding its concept, structure and differentiation from centralized architectures is crucial for understanding the innovation of blockchain technology.

While P2P networks are the technical foundation of blockchain systems, virtual machines greatly increase the functionality of blockchain systems as they allow non-censorable and autonomous programs (in the form of smart contracts) to be uploaded onto a blockchain. This is the basis of what some refer to as the Web 3.0. Blockchain is said to complement the current state of the internet by an increased connectivity through direct connections between users, new concepts of ownership, the uniqueness of digital assets and un-intermediated exchange. It adds another layer for payments, decentralized applications, automated and autonomous organizations, which need no central coordinator. By covering the topics of virtual machines and the smart contracts they enable we account for the technical evolution which the technology has experienced in the last years. Numerous applications (Chapter 4) and social impacts (Chapter 3), which we will focus on in the course of this book, rely on the increased functionality of blockchains through virtual machines. This is why we provide a detailed description of how they work and of the smart contracts they enable.

Second, the mathematical components of blockchain technology are explained. These include elliptic-curve cryptography, which underpins hash algorithms – an essential part in blockchain systems – and

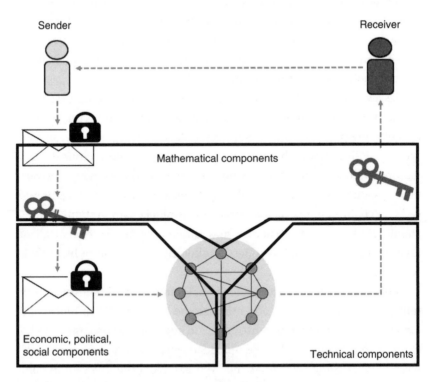

Figure 2.1 Basic components of blockchain technology

public-key cryptography. Understanding the functionality of hash algorithms and how they are employed in blockchain systems is crucial, because they allow for the encryption and compression of data as well as verification schemes in blockchains' maintenance processes. Not only do hash algorithms enable the efficient compression of transaction data and their verification, but they also play a crucial role in the economic incentivization of miners for validating transactions and blocks. Without hash algorithms, blockchains would not exist in the form they do, nor would they be functional without public-key cryptography. Public-key cryptography allows for the pseudonymity[1] of participants and lays the mathematical foundation of interaction and verification processes in the network. It is important to understand public-key cryptography and how it is applied in blockchain systems, as it enables direct ownership and control of digital blockchain assets, which further facilitates censorship resistance and potentially new marketplaces, for example, for personal data access or personal preferences. Before we dig deeper into the discussion, it is of importance to understand how these mathematical components work. This not only fosters the understanding of how social impact is created, but also enables the readers to assess the potentials themselves.

Third, we identify the prerequisite for freely accessible and transparent blockchain systems to be economic, social and political concepts: blockchains employ consensus mechanisms, which allow a network of participants to continuously agree on the state of a database, the manipulation of which could be extremely attractive financially. For example, the consensus mechanism employed in Bitcoin is thereby highly scalable in terms of user increases. Since consensus mechanisms have been researched for decades and play such a special role in

---

1. The term "pseudonymity" (short for pseudo-anonymity) refers to the fact that although addresses are alphanumerical codes and no personal information needs to be public in any form for the functionality and participation in the network, interacting with a known person reveals the identity behind an address. Moreover, the transparent nature of the blockchain allows one to view any validated transaction ever conducted in the network. In combination with other data, forensics allow for assigning identities to addresses.

blockchains, a brief historic review is provided on the topic. Moreover, as blockchain systems are potentially capable of widespread adoption, the question arises how they can be governed. Especially, given that blockchain systems promise to be decentralized and un-intermediated. The topic of governance in information technology (IT) has been subject to research since the early days of computer science and the governance of a decentralized organization poses substantial challenges. That is, beneficial governance is crucial for a network to adapt to a changing environment and evolve technically. An important aspect of governance is the incentivization to use a particular software or IT system in the way it was initially intended. Incentivization in a decentralized network of individuals plays an important role in the securitization of a blockchain. Accordingly, we will return in some detail to the question and practicalities of incentivization in P2P networks and blockchain systems. Understanding how such community-owned networks are governed provides the reader with the foundational understanding of how blockchain can provide individuals with higher degrees of freedom to choose which (political, financial or social) system they want to belong to. We will dig deeper into the discussion on how blockchain (re-)empowers the individual in Chapter 4.

2.1 TECHNICAL COMPONENTS

The major technical component of a blockchain in its pure form is a P2P network, a technical layer over the internet, which facilitates the interconnectivity of network participants. P2P networks are characterized by direct connections between peers and flat hierarchies, in which every peer is equipped with the same rights and duties in the network. The purpose of creating networks of peers with equal status is to ensure the network's functionality despite high fluctuation of peers and external threats to the maintenance of the network – dependencies are reduced while resilience and performance are increased. For a comprehensive understanding of the societal value of this architecture, a brief historic review and comparison to client–server architecture and grid architecture follows. Recognizing the different technical architectures that characterize today's internet as we know it helps us to appreciate the true innovation of blockchain technology.

Blockchain systems like Bitcoin can have the sole purpose of providing a cryptographically secure and un-intermediated digital form of cash – internet money. However, some blockchain systems have extended functionalities through an implemented virtual machine. Such technical implementations allow for programming, uploading and executing code on a blockchain. Since the transfer of valuable assets and electronic cash has so far usually been intermediated, a freely accessible infrastructure for applications, which initiate transactions in an autonomous, automated, distributed and un-intermediated way, is a potential game-changer for society, as it redesigns interaction between individuals. Accordingly, the technical component of a virtual machine and the concept of smart contracts are also highlighted in this chapter.

Peer-to-peer networks

Basically, peer-to-peer (P2P) describes direct communication between computers. Unlike central systems, in which a server processes and distributes all information, P2P communication takes place directly between users of equal status.

P2P constitutes a design pattern that resulted from a network architecture evolution, following the client–server and grid architectures. In contrast to centralized client–server relationships, "P2P networks are decentralized distributed systems that enable computers to share and integrate their computing resources, data and services" (Liu & Antonopoulos 2010: 73). The basic concept is that the decentralization of network architecture enables the creation of networks with fewer dependencies, greater resilience and higher capacities than centralized architectures. High levels of decentralization thereby consist of a set of benefits and potential problems compared to centralized structures. Decentralized networks can be more beneficial in specific settings, while centralized architectures are more advantageous in others. For example, in central systems there are single-point-of-failure risks due to hacks, which are however countered by higher system speed, since only one central instance has to process and coordinate transactions. While there is no single-point-of-failure risk with decentralized networks, the speed of data processing is often lower.

Decentralization and centralization constitute the maximum and minimum end points in a continuum of network architectures, which encompasses hybrid models of P2P and client–server architectures. When designing network architectures for specific applications, there is an inherent trade-off between performance, control, accessibility, resilience and dependencies. In the following, client–server, grid and P2P architectures and their different sets of characteristics are introduced. The comparison of these architecture models highlights the advantageous characteristics of P2P networks and leads the way to understanding the actual core invention of blockchain technology.

Client–server architecture

Large elements of today's internet are based on client–server architecture, including the great parts of the web and email. From a consumer's perspective, increasingly important and established online companies such as Facebook, Google and Amazon employ client–server architectures to facilitate their services and social network's functionality. Client–server architectures in this setting are generally not inferior to P2P architectures. They are efficient in handling specific computational and economic settings. Computationally, they are able to handle and manage access to and maintain control over their most important resources efficiently. Economically, they help to protect companies' interests and business models by establishing data silos and restrictions for the use of their service.

In a traditional client–server relationship, contents and services are stored and provided on a single server or set of servers. Clients are able to access the contents and services by sending requests to the server. By entering a website domain, the visitor (client) sends an access request to

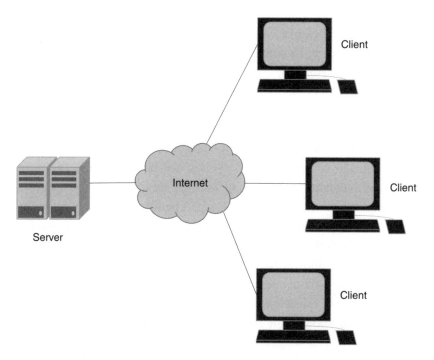

Figure 2.2 Client–server architecture

Source: adapted from Liu & Antonopoulos (2010: 72).

the server, on which the website's content is stored. The website builds upon the data packages sent by the server. Similarly, a cloud service is accessed by a client who is able to technically prove a permission (with a fee or token).

The centralized structure of client–server architectures can be disadvantageous under specific circumstances: in order to be able to provide contents and services continuously, the server-side resources must be sufficient. Server-side limitations encompass network bandwidth, central processing unit (CPU) capability, input/output speed and storage space. As a consequence, limited technical resources may result in a lack of capacity to handle more than a certain number of requests at a time. Ensuring the capability of one's servers to handle problematic circumstances, the provider faces high costs, which contributes to establishing a base price for the content or service. A more fundamental shortcoming of centralized technical architecture relates to the uniqueness of a server and the provision of its contents and services. Once availability and accessibility are disrupted there is no alternative for clients to request certain content or service. This problem in client–server relationships is referred to as a single point of failure. A failure can result from internal or external activity. The provision of contents and services through a single server can be threatened by numerous attack vectors. The potential damage of compromised servers can be enormous. The most publicized incidents usually entail sensitive data being retrieved from compromised servers and getting into the hands of criminals willing to sell or misuse it. Moreover, damage can result from the manipulation of data and technical interference of the content's or service's availability (Liu & Antonopoulos 2010). Compromised servers and data are a persistent characteristic of our time. On a regular basis, data silos are technically drained of valuable information which leads to big data breaches including well-known companies, such as Yahoo (2013), Ebay (2014), T-Mobile (2015), LinkedIn (2016), Uber (2016), Equifax (2017), Facebook (2018) among many others. These data breaches include leaked personal information of customers, who voluntarily and because of a lack of alternatives, provide their data to these companies to use a specific service. Centrally stored data and contents are then exposed to attacks that specifically target centralized structures. Centralized client–server relationships are characterized by the inherent dependency of clients towards a particular server and provider which involves clients' trust towards the integrity of provided contents and services. Hence, a client–server relationship always involves trust from the client's perspective about the correctness of the relevant data, maintenance and security.

The fact that such data breaches occur regularly and have not become less frequent over time can be interpreted as an indication that the current systems are problematic and that new systems should be developed that can minimize or exclude those risks. Blockchain technology presents one approach, in which databases are distributed and data is encrypted and tamper-proof. The technical and mathematical components allow for digital rights management, which is user-centric in the sense that personal data is securely owned (and access can be granted selectively) by the individual it belongs to (see Chapter 4 on self-sovereign identities).

Grid-architecture

Grid architectures refer to client–server structure for distributed computing that supports flexible, secure and coordinated resource-sharing among virtual organizations. Virtual organizations are dynamic collections of individuals and institutions, whose grid forms a high-performance computing and data infrastructure (Liu & Antonopoulos 2010). Grid architecture focuses on facilitating interoperability among resource providers and users to offer access to substantial resources regardless of geographical distances. It was first used in academia and in scientific communities to allow high-performance super computers, massive storage space, sensors, satellites, software applications, and data belonging to different institutions to be connected through the internet. Grid computing describes the clustering of computers (resources) in a network to perform specific resource-intensive tasks.

Establishing an increased technical interconnectivity of participants in grid architectures is necessary for combining and providing the functionality of the shared network resources. This does not mean that interconnectivity between all participants is necessary. Rather than connecting each network participant with one another, grid architecture is more about clustering, so that combined resources (e.g. servers) can be used by individual users or groups (clients) (see Figure 2.3). Consequently, a grid architecture is characterized by a distributed rather than a decentralized infrastructure of clients and servers, established to harness combined resources, while the coordination and processing tasks are conducted by a central entity.

In contrast to traditional client–server architectures, distributed and decentralized architectures can be differentiated at an infrastructure level and at a processing level. The infrastructure describes direct technical connections between participants, whereas processing encompasses tasks of routing, searching and coordinating. Traditional grid

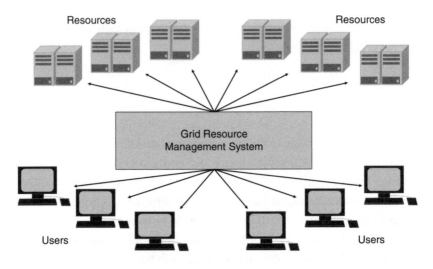

Figure 2.3 Grid computing environment

Source: adapted from Ku-Mahamud & Nasir (2010: 40).

architecture combines the resources of network participants to perform resource intensive tasks jointly, so it is decentralized to a certain extent at a technical level, but the coordination is performed centrally by a trusted intermediary. Most forms of grid architecture share this characteristic of a central entity, which processes requests and performs the agglomeration and coordination of resources from the available capacity combined in the network.

What accompanies the concept of virtual organizations and centralized coordination in grid architectures is access restrictions and dependence on the operability of the central entity. Grid architectures are commonly not run by an agglomeration of participants (and their resources) following the same pre-agreed principles and guidelines. The entity for performing the routing and coordination functions is established in a centralized manner, because participants of such networks form a trusted setup in which a centralized management of requests and operations is the most efficient modus operandi. In such trust-environments, there is no advantage in sharing the processing and routing with a subset of, or all, network participants. The interests of all participants are aligned towards efficiently harnessing the network's resources.

A grid architecture with access open to everybody in need of excessive computing power would be a great achievement. But challenges would remain, especially if every participant were allowed to offer their personal resources to the network, which would result in enormous volatility of available capacity and challenges in terms of organization and coordination. Moreover, the dependencies of users towards the accessibility and accuracy of operation, functionality and accounting would be high. There are start-ups that are pursuing the harnessing of blockchain technology to decentralize the coordinator's tasks: they operate access-free networks for performing resource-intensive computing tasks through the available capacities of all participants (who are incentivized to provide their resources), without a trusted centralized organizer. Projects like Golem (2016), SONM (2017) and iExec (2018) are decentralized and are opening up distributed computing networks to everybody – other than closed networks of corporate or university servers, for example. The advantage of decentralizing the central coordinator is that a network is established in which everybody can request computing power, for example, while others get paid to rent their computing resources. The blockchain thereby acts as the immutable database for recording transactions and proof of operation – the accounting-layer for resource-sharing. The auditability of the blockchain creates a trusted setup without a central entity on which to rely.

P2P architecture

The term "P2P" refers to the technical connections between participants ("peers") in a P2P network on the infrastructure level, in which the sum of connections forms a network. The term "peer" implies that there is no hierarchy among the participants in the network – they are each equipped with the same rights and duties. P2P systems provide a virtual network environment, which is a logical overlay network over a

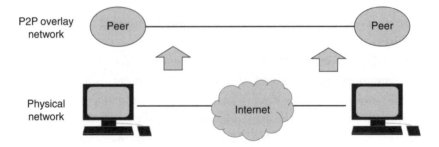

Figure 2.4 P2P architecture

Source: adapted from Liu & Antonopoulos (2010).

physical infrastructure (see Figure 2.4). P2P networks have experienced a huge increase in popularity in the last two decades, such that they have become an important part of today's internet. P2P network architectures are employed in applications for instant messaging, Voice over IP[2], streaming, resource-intense computing, search engines and file-sharing.

In contrast to centralized client–server architectures, P2P architectures do not rely on centralized servers to provide contents or services, but each node in the network acts simultaneously as a client and a server. This way, P2P architectures can greatly increase the utilization of collective resources at the edge of the internet, such as information, bandwidth and computing resources. Each peer is constantly routing queries and serving resources for other nodes (Liu & Antonopoulos 2010). A network of participants interacts and shares its collective resources in order to improve an overall network's performance, which makes it advantageous for every user.

Other than in grid architectures, an increased interconnectivity is generally favourable for the performance of P2P networks. The more connections are established in P2P networks, the faster it can perform, the more capabilities it has and the more resilient it becomes. They

---

2. Voice over Internet Protocol (VoIP) describes the transmission of voice and multimedia over the internet infrastructure using specialized protocols. This contrasts voice transmission over traditional telephone networks.

scale performance with a greater network of connections, while for grid architectures, an increased interconnectivity among users and providers brings no advantage – connections are distributed to the extent that is most favourable. In sum, P2P networks are more decentralized at the infrastructure level.

In comparison to users who want to share resources with others through a central-server architecture, P2P networks enable users to directly retrieve and share resources with connected peers. This way dependencies for users are decreased, as no external central server is necessary in this setting. From an economic point of view, the tasks of a server setup and maintenance as well as the securing of server capabilities are distributed across all participants. Moreover, the technical tasks and responsibilities of service provision are distributed across the network, which eliminates the bottleneck of centralized servers and increases the performance of the network. P2P networks theoretically exploit bandwidth, processing power and storage space of all participants, whose overall capability thereby increases in flexibility. Under the assumption of the same costs occurring for a single service provider and a network of peers as service providers, the realized performance increase of the P2P architecture results in efficiency gains for the network. Moreover, advantageous features of P2P architectures encompass the diminishing of a single point of failure, hence reduced dependency and a more resilient service provision. The availability of the service or content is ensured through redundant service provision of multiple connected peers in case of hardware or software failures, or any other failures of single peers in the network (Liu & Antonopoulos 2010).

Figure 2.5 illustrates the exemplary process of a file transfer across a P2P network. A requester spreads a request across the network. Information is passed from peer to peer and arrives (in this case via two other peers) at a provider that has the appropriate file. Subsequently, the provider transmits the file directly to the requester without having to call in other network participants again.

At the processing level, P2P architectures can be classified by their degree of centralization – they can be based on centralized, decentralized or hybrid networks (Liu & Antonopoulos 2010; Figure 2.6). The degree of

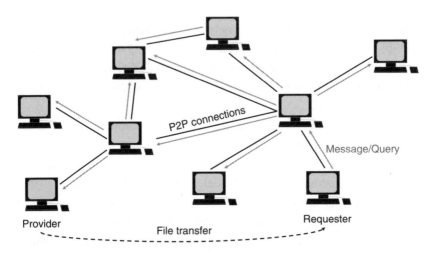

Figure 2.5 Message broadcasting across the Gnutella network

Source: adapted from Liu & Antonopoulos (2010).

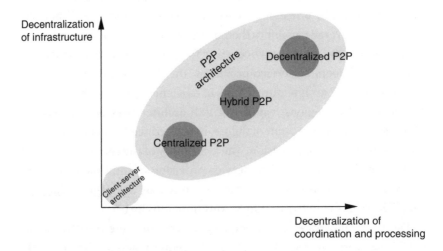

Figure 2.6 The dimensions of decentralization in P2P network architectures

centralization refers to a P2P network's necessity of employing a central server, used to conduct certain tasks in order to ensure a network's functionality. An example of a centralized P2P network is one of the first file sharing networks, Napster, for which a central server was employed to fulfil a routing and search function: the centralized Napster server kept the list of peers and their respective lists of files to be shared. A search request from a user seeking to source a specific file was directed towards and responded to by the central server, while the actual file transfer took place directly between the peers. Between the two peers, one of which takes the role of the provider with the requested file on their personal server, the other one is the client. From there, more sophisticated models of centralized P2P networks emerged, such as BitTorrent for which a more efficient file transfer protocol was implemented breaking up files into smaller fragments for transmission from different peer nodes. However, centralized P2P networks partly face the same problems as client–server and grid architectures, as the central server provides a vital function to the network and presents a single point of failure.

Decentralized P2P networks have managed to reduce the physical necessity of a central server by implementing protocols for peer node discovery and distributed search and transmissions. In contrast to centralized P2P systems, the routing functions can be distributed across all participants and implemented in the client software, as in Gnutella. In Gnutella, a search query is propagated by a user through its client software across all connected peers. As connected peers have a different set of connections, the search query is distributed across the whole network in the best case, while every receiving peer automatically checks, if the required file is to be found in their storage. Eventually, a search query can be responded to positively by a node, which results in a file transfer between providing peer(s) and the client (see Figure 2.5). In Gnutella, the advantages of P2P networks have been successfully implemented, reaching a beneficial state in terms of efficiency and resilience compared to centralized architectures. However, the cost of a decentralized system is a high volume of search queries across the network, due to inefficient or redundant routing tasks – the price for the network's resiliency and users' independence.

The evolution of P2P network architectures is a crucial and major forerunner of blockchain technology. The invention of Bitcoin and consequently the first implementation of a blockchain can be considered a logical evolutionary step forward for P2P application and the entire internet. P2P network architecture forms the technical foundation for blockchain systems, while blockchain technology enhances P2P architecture by establishing a unique and verifiable database, incentivization schemes and mechanisms for efficiently distributing the tasks of processing as well as the mechanisms for creating consensus about the validity of the exchange of unique (digital) assets. In a P2P system, the successful result of its operation may be the completed provision of a requested file, for example, a file assembled and downloaded through numerous peers. The file is then the reproduction of an existing file. The P2P infrastructure of blockchain systems, on the other hand, is for exchanging information about state changes – such as the transfer of digital assets. The decentralized database of blockchains enables the creation of a P2P network, whose purpose is not the replication and sharing of resources, but the exchange of unique resources or assets. This includes the requirement to keep the majority of the network in concordance with the state of the assets' distribution (the actual state of the database). This requirement differentiates blockchain networks from traditional decentralized P2P networks: a mechanism is established to create consensus among all participants about the actual state of distribution, which changes with every newly validated transfer. Moreover, a mechanism is established, which verifies transfer requests and separates valid from invalid ones.

Blockchain systems implement P2P architecture (with varying levels of decentralization) at the infrastructure level to technically establish direct connections among the peers in a network, enabling transactions of assets to be initiated without an intermediary. A transaction is technically a request propagated across the network by its initiator that seeks verification. A valid request results in a change of ownership in the blockchain database, which is also propagated across the network. Because the blockchain database changes continuously with every transfer, every participant actively verifies the correctness (verifiability) of the newly propagated set of transactions (blocks). Invalid data gets rejected and is not passed on to connecting peers. The P2P architecture allows for the effective distribution of transfer requests and blocks in the network, to keep every participant up to date. This creates latency because of physical distances of network participants. A central party would be able to perform this task faster but presents an undesirable single point of failure. For propagating messages, Bitcoin for example uses the proprietary gossip protocol to distribute messages across the network as quickly as possible. For this purpose, the protocol obliges each peer to pass on the respective information to each directly connected peer: the fastest possible method for disseminating information about the network's consensus.

Virtual machines and smart contracts

A virtual machine is the run-time environment for applications and programs – it acts as a virtual computer and the engine within which transaction code is executed. Numerous blockchain systems have implemented virtual machines in their system design so as to form a network of distributed virtual machines. Virtual machines greatly increase the functionalities of blockchains. Their implementation enables programs and applications to be run, whose code is irreversibly submitted and transparently settled on the blockchain. These programs are commonly referred to as smart contracts. They basically present scripts on a blockchain, tied to specific accounts with corresponding addresses. Virtual machines are not or do not have to be executed by every user of a blockchain, but only by full nodes, in other words network participants who store the complete transaction history of the blockchain and possibly also validate them.

Each node which runs a virtual machine redundantly performs applications and programs that have been submitted to the blockchain. Thus, executable code can be implemented on a decentralized system so that everybody can review and trigger it by sending transactions to the contracts' addresses. Every participant in a blockchain network is able to verify and execute this code, as well as review its transaction log. Each time a transaction triggers a program, the code is run by the distributed virtual machine.

Potentially every node in the network has a virtual machine implemented in its client software. By redundantly distributing virtual machines onto every network participant, all of them can agree on executing the same instructions. This means that every program which has been submitted and triggered is run redundantly by all network participants. Every time a peer interacts with the smart contract, the respective validating node executes the code once again using the virtual machine. This is necessary for the holistic concept of a blockchain: because smart contracts are triggered by transactions and commonly initiate transactions according to certain conditions, their code needs to be run by every node redundantly as part of the consensus mechanism. The price for executing programs on a decentralized infrastructure without central intermediaries is the inefficiency created by redundantly performed computations in the course of finding consensus by the majority of the network participants. These are the costs of using and maintaining a decentralized, censorship-resistant and non-intermediated network.

In the case of Ethereum, a contract is created when a transaction is sent to an empty address with the code as additional transaction data. The Ethereum virtual machine (EVM) interprets the event, creates an account and "stores" the embedded code. Potentially, such contracts act as sole entities whose code can be triggered by sending a transaction to its address. They can also present the transactional backbone for web applications with user interfaces – so-called decentralized applications (dapps).

Smart contracts are agreements, formalized into code and stored in the blockchain. The term "smart contract" was coined by Nick Szabo in 1997 to describe the idea of automated and verifiable contract execution via code (Szabo 1997). Blockchain technology did not exist when Szabo wrote his article; however, blockchain, or a secure decentralized way of transacting value, presents the infrastructure for running these. Smart contracts are verifiable because they are deployed on the blockchain – they cannot be manipulated after an agreement has been set. Moreover, they can be a potentially cost-efficient method for conducting transactions, for example, replacing notary services or ownership transactions. In principle, the term "smart contract" is not particularly suitable to describe the applied concept, as it does not have to be a (legal) contract. Rather, it is computer code stored on the blockchain that can be executed de-centrally, and once executed, runs pre-defined actions, in other words transactions. It can thus be regarded as being the automated executor of a contract. This can follow simple logic (e.g. if a transaction occurs, execute a new transaction – a forwarding logic) or a complex system. For example, decentralized autonomous organizations (DAOs) can be programmed that react and operate on the basis of incoming transactions. An example for this is MakerDAO, a decentralized system, which enables a so-called "stable coin" (a decentralized cryptocurrency, which is pegged to a value of $1) and whose governance is conducted by the community.

The computational capacities of blockchain virtual machines and the ability of smart contracts to call and trigger other smart contracts means that constructs of code can be created with increasingly complex logic. Consequently, there is a huge potential for smart contracts and public blockchain systems to become the foundation for a new type of app, characterized by un-intermediated interactions for businesses and the consumers. Consumers' trust in an app shifts from trust in a company's integrity to the verifiable computer code of a dapp (decentralized app). We will return to this discussion and the social implications of automated interactions in Chapter 3.

Deploying and running a smart contract is associated with costly computational efforts, which validators are compensated for. That is, the more complex the computational effort of running a smart contract is, the more costly it is for the creator to deploy it and for the user to trigger and make use of it. The payment for deploying smart contracts on the Ethereum network is directed to the node, which stores, computes, executes and verifies the submitted code. Accordingly, for a user, using a dapp rather than a comparable app, the interaction can be more expensive. But instead of being dependent on a third party (e.g. payment provider), which intermediates the payment process and thus adds costs for the provider and the user, using a dapp ensures that no costs of an intermediary arise.

The virtual machine adds an abstraction layer to blockchain networks, whose purpose is the exchange of value. Bitcoin's functionality is limited compared to those networks which have a virtual machine implemented. But in contrast to Ethereum or EOS, Bitcoin's invention was not due to the creation of a network of extended functionalities and automation. Rather, Bitcoin's innovation was the creation of an internet-based currency, which is not controlled by a central entity and consequently reduces or removes dependencies of owners on the functionality, availability and supply volatility of traditional currency. Due to technical shortcomings, Bitcoin has become an alternative financial asset, comparable to gold (in digital form), rather than being a currency with high velocity. However, this may change in the future, when scalability solutions potentially enable Bitcoin to be used as a means of payment.

Technical summary

The architectures of client–server, grid and P2P can be differentiated across two main dimensions: (1) the infrastructure level and (2) the processing level. Each architecture can be regarded as a specific arrangement of trade-offs. On the one hand, more centralized technical infrastructures can be more efficient in terms of performance and control. On the other hand, the more centralized a technical infrastructure is, the more threats it faces for manipulation, censorship and technical attack vectors. Consequently, technical designs vary and offer certain trade-offs, which encompass but are not limited to performance speed versus independence on central providers, resilience and availability of a service provision versus performance speed and control, as well as access control versus censorship resistance.

The technical P2P infrastructure of public blockchains is commonly decentralized on a technical level, as well as the processing tasks associated with transferring assets. These processing tasks include the propagation of new transfer requests and blocks, as well as their verification and validation. The participants in a network are actively propagating transactions (after verification processes) until the requests reach specific participants, who perform tasks of block formation. Block formation includes the validation of a request and its inclusion into the blockchain database. The amended blockchain database is propagated across the network the same way as a transfer request. If a majority of the network participants find no conflict in the process of verifying the amended blockchain, the amended blockchain constitutes the state of the distribution and the transfer request is finally conducted. There are more processing tasks for finding such consensus, for example, who is allowed to form blocks. These will be examined in the section on consensus (Section 2.3).

P2P systems allow the formation of networks which are connected over the internet in a borderless fashion. They are also hard to regulate, as they are comparable to swarms of individuals who cooperate on fulfilling the respective network's purpose. This makes P2P technology powerful in terms of creating independence of individuals from central third-parties and strengthens the resilience of a network against participant fluctuation and regulation. This enhances an individual's freedom of choice, a topic we will refer to in detail in Chapter 3.

In combination with virtual machines and smart contracts, blockchain systems become even more powerful, as potentially many more uses can be realized on blockchain infrastructures that are freely accessible. Imagine millions of unbanked people getting access to financial markets and being able to invest in start-ups and index funds, receiving credit based on fair and incorruptible credit risk evaluations or collecting international funding for the local economy, which is paid out automatically in tranches based on achieving milestones of a pre-defined roadmap. How blockchain can contribute to this idea is subject to a dedicated section on capital markets and ICOs in Chapter 4.

2.2 MATHEMATICAL COMPONENTS

Blockchain technology is based on various mathematical and cryptographic components: elliptic-curve cryptography (ECC) and hashing,

Merkle trees and public-key cryptography. The importance of the components is that they facilitate a certain level of anonymity for users in the network. The mathematical components allow for operating the network with mutual control, without the necessity to reveal user identities. The assembly of blockchains' mathematical components provide features such as an individual's sovereignty over their digitized identity and data (see Chapters 3 and 4). Cryptography lays the ground for privacy and censorship resistance, topics which are growing in importance in today's increasingly digitized society. This chapter sets out how blockchain offers a suitable infrastructure for disruptive identity management, privacy enhancement and censorship resistance, focusing on the functionalities of cryptography and the applied methods in blockchain systems.

Cryptography is a method for encrypting and decrypting information using complex mathematics. Starting from an unencrypted piece of information, such as a text file, mathematical algorithms (ciphers) create a new piece of information (code) from the original information, which is completely useless for a receiver unless it is decrypted. The code is thereby derived from the original piece of information, which creates a mathematical relationship to both the code and the unencrypted information. The cipher depicts this relation for the receiver, so that only receivers who know about this relationship are able to decrypt the information. One of the earliest ciphers was used in military communication of Caesar's army: each letter was substituted by a letter three spaces to the left in the alphabet. This ensured the protection of crucial military secrets in correspondence, as only specific individuals knew the cipher to decrypt the message.

Hash algorithms

A hash algorithm is a computational transformation of data that involves an iterative compression function. In general, a hash function performs the transformation of data of arbitrary size into a fixed size (Stalling

Table 2.1 Outputs of pre-selected hash algorithms

Algorithm	Input	Output[1]
SHA 256[2]	HelloWorld	872e4e50ce9990d8b041330c47c9ddd11bec6b503 ae9386a99da8584e9bb12c4
SHA 256	HelloWorld1	90b46dd6fad0a8db496945a6be27d95fbb7860482 235697056b89b1d0783685e
Keccak-224	HelloWorld	7fd2a6ffc807105a47a559b5c8043f42bb7dbfc3b76 bceb8d1e603f4
Keccak-224	HelloWorld1	27a7c239e4778594a4d6696c30dadfa1fa5998500e 311d047eee4a76

[1] Hashes generated from https://emn178.github.io/online-tools/index.html (accessed 12 April 2020).

[2] SHA 256 (Secure Hash Algorithm with an output of 256 bits).

2011). The fixed-size output length is an indicator of the difficulty of its reproduction. The most widely used hash functions in cryptography are so-called Secure Hash Algorithms (SHA).

As shown in Table 2.1, the SHA 256 transforms the input "HelloWorld" into a string of alphanumeric code. The length of the output is fixed, no matter the size of the input. A slightly changed input ("HelloWorld1") results in a completely different output. The same hash output can only be reproduced by the input it is derived from. Following these properties, hashing presents a tool for compressing and indexing data – hash algorithms are typically used to provide a digital fingerprint of a file's content (Kessler 2016). The principle objective of hash functions is data integrity (Stallings 2011). A manipulated file can be discovered, if the file under review and the original file are hashed with the same algorithm. If the output of the reviewed file does not match the original file's hash output, it can be concluded that the file has been tampered with.

Cryptographic hash functions are applied in security domains. It is computationally infeasible to decrypt a hash so as to identify the data that was hashed or find data which results in the same hash. That is why the process of hashing (applying hash algorithms) is commonly also referred to as one-way encryption (Kessler 2016). The relevant properties of cryptographic hash functions can be identified as one-way property and collision-free property (Stallings 2011):

- One way-property: a data set of random size can be hashed into a fixed-length hash value. It is infeasible to derive the data set from a hash value;
- Collision-free property: it is statistically feasible, but extremely unlikely that two different data sets result in the same hash value.

These properties come from the application of elliptic-curve multiplication, which is based on the discrete logarithm problem. Elliptic-curve cryptography has increasingly displaced other cryptographic approaches because it offers higher security levels than other forms. The main applications for SHA algorithms are digital signatures, hashed message authentication code, key generation, and pseudorandom number generation (Stallings 2011).

Hash algorithms are crucial components of public blockchain systems and are applied extensively for encryption purposes as well as for data compression:

- Public-key cryptography: public and private keys, addresses, and digital signatures are derived via cryptographic hash functions (see next chapter);
- Mining: the repeated submission (brute-force) of hashes via the "hashcash" cost function while changing a variable (nonce) in the hashed data each time describes the mathematical task in which miners compete;
- Hashed block headers facilitate the chaining of blocks through including the hash of the preceding block in a hash of the following block;
- Verification: to find out if a data set has been altered, the data set can be hashed, and the resulting hash value needs to be identical to the provided hash value.

Public-key cryptography is a form of asymmetric encryption, which allows encrypted communication to be created that has public and shareable keys. The key structure of private and public keys is crucial in blockchain systems, as their application forms the basis for a system of verifiable balances. As public-key cryptography forms an integral part of blockchain technology, which is described in greater depth in the following chapter.

Mining refers to a mechanism for finding out which network participant has created a new block that extends the existing blockchain with recently initiated and valid transactions. The hash algorithm SHA256 is applied to create a brute-force task for network participants, who are not only using the network but dedicating computation capacity by verifying transactions and forming blocks. Each miner verifies incoming transactions, collects valid transactions in a transaction pool and forms a candidate block including the transactions from their individual pool. The newly formed blocks are hashed with a single adjustable variable, called a nonce, until the resulting hash meets specific criteria. The nonce is changed for every hash until a value is found that creates the desired hash of the block. This repetitive computational task is conducted by numerous network participants who have an economic incentive (block reward) to find a hash before all other miners. The statistical feasibility of finding desired hashes are dependent on the computing power that is provided by an entity. Mining is part of the consensus algorithm of open blockchain networks.

As hashes present fingerprints of digital data, hashing in blockchain networks is applied to create fingerprints of blocks. In the processes of mining for new blocks, the block-specific fingerprint of the previous block is included, which facilitates a computational chaining of blocks (see Figure 2.7). The chaining of blocks creates a coherent chain whose relationships can be verified by everyone in the network. As the body of a block includes transactions, transactions are chained so that a verifiable transaction path of the transacted assets is created. Rather than a verifiable path of transactions, a verifiable table of distribution is provided, based on the data inherent to the blockchain.

In the course of propagating newly initiated and incoming transactions, the process of verification, which is performed by every participant

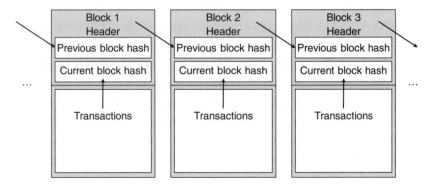

Figure 2.7 Simplified blockchain cryptographic chaining

Source: adapted from Pan *et al.* (2018).

prior to sending the transaction information to every connected peer, is composed of the verification of hashes. The validity of a transaction is checked through verifying the existence and capacity of a sender's and receiver's address through the available blockchain data. In the course of propagating newly created and incoming candidate blocks, which include validated transactions, every participant can verify the validity of the block, i.e. that the hash meets the desired criteria, because the input information as well as the cipher is provided by the propagator. While the required nonce for finding the desired block hash is extremely hard to find, its verification is an easy computational task. This way the maximum level of transparency for transactions is ensured, so that everyone can check for the validity of transaction data.

Moreover, the characteristic of hashing algorithms for compressing data is crucial in creating blockchains, because they reduce the data load to the minimum that is necessary. This refers to the process of chaining blocks using only hashes of previous blocks, as well as shortening the processes of verification through block hashes and transaction hashes. This leads us to the concept of Merkle trees.

Merkle trees are data structures used for efficiently summarizing large data sets, while allowing for easy verification processes for the integrity of the data (Antonopoulos 2015). As visualized in Figure 2.8, a tree-like structure results from summarizing data from different

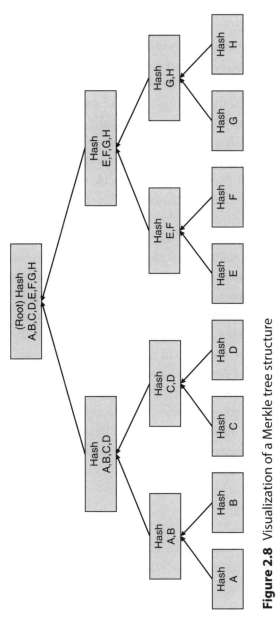

Figure 2.8 Visualization of a Merkle tree structure

Source: adapted from Antonopoulos (2015).

branches. In blockchain technology, Merkle trees are used from the bottom up, to create a single hash that serves as a fingerprint for all transactions included in a block. The single hash results from the structured hashing of transactions, which are hashed in pairs until a single hash, the Merkle root, is calculated. This structure eases the verification, if a transaction is included in a block.

Through the application of cryptographic means in the creation of a record in the form of blockchains, the integrity of past data is ensured. Tampering with past data is theoretically possible, but the inherent security mechanisms make manipulation economically inefficient. Manipulating a transaction in a past block requires the recalculation of any concluding block to make the manipulated transaction fit with the concluding transactions as well as the calculation efforts to create valid hashes of concluding blocks. This is computationally expensive, which generates more costs than benefit for the manipulator. Moreover, a manipulator needs to convince the network, more accurately a majority of a network, to accept the manipulated chain as the valid chain and start dedicating computational resources in the maintenance of the new chain. While these procedures are continuously conducted automatically for client software, a manipulated chain would become apparent in a transparent blockchain ecosystem. Using the example of Bitcoin, a manipulator needs to top up his relative computational power or convince network participants up to a minimum of 51 per cent of all computational power to conduct a successful attack. As of 15 April 2019, the overall hash rate of Bitcoin comprises 46,080,845 TH/s,[3] which imposes a massive security wall for Bitcoin's blockchain.

Public-key cryptography

Caesar's cipher (in which letters in a word are substituted by another in the alphabet) is an example of symmetric encryption. The cipher

---

3. TH/s is short for terahashes per second. Performing one terahash each second means a hash, as shown in Table 2.1, is being performed 1,000,000,000,000 times a second using different inputs.

used is both the encryption and decryption method (see Figure 2.9). Symmetric encryption has several shortcomings, as the cipher needs to be known to both sender and receiver. The sender gives away the encryption key, because it is necessary for the receiver to decrypt the message. Consequently, sender and receiver need to agree in advance upon the cipher they use, either in a physical meeting or through a secure channel. Today's encryption methods are far more complex and sophisticated.

Public-key cryptography, which is also referred to as asymmetric cryptography, is an essential invention in computer and information security. It describes cryptographic applications that involve the use of private and public keys to encrypt messages, while ensuring that the message can only be decrypted by its addressee. It is innovative compared to symmetric encryption, as it introduces key management. Through its structure involving a publicly shared and a private key, encrypted communication can take place between receiver and sender who are unknown to each other, as well as without prior communication (Salomaa 2013). A public key is shared and accessible to anyone, while the private key is secret. The public key is mathematically derived from the private key. A receiver of a message can use the public key of a sender to verify whether it has been sent by the sender, specifically, whether the message has been manipulated during transit.

The decryption of a message is conducted through a combination of a user's public and private key. Figure 2.10 shows how asymmetric cryptography works in a simplified way: the sender uses a recipient's public key to encrypt their message. Moreover, a sender signs the message with their private key, thereby producing a digital signature that allows the recipient to verify the integrity of the data. The encrypted message is forwarded to the recipient, who is then able to decrypt the message using their own private key. The mathematical connection of private and public keys ensures that the message can only be read by the addressee, as long as the recipient's private key is kept secret. This presents a major benefit compared to symmetric cryptography in the context of messaging. Public keys allow messages to be directed to specific addressees, while it is computationally infeasible to extract a

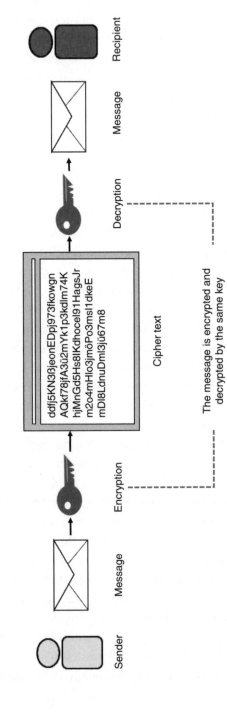

Figure 2.9 Visualization of symmetric cryptography for messaging

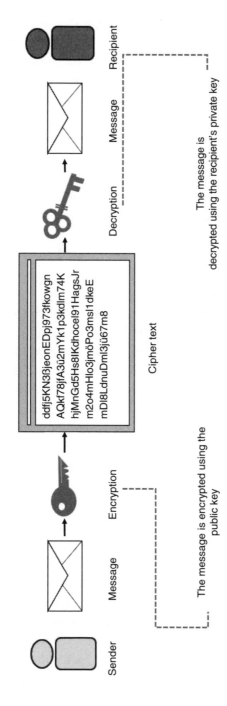

Figure 2.10 Visualization of asymmetric cryptography for messaging

corresponding private key from a publicly shared key. It is computationally easy to generate a private, and the corresponding public key, but it is practically impossible to derive the private key from the public key. This is because public-key cryptography uses the intractability of certain mathematical problems (prime-number exponentiation and elliptic-curve multiplication). This feature of public-key cryptography is used to facilitate an architectural foundation for trustless network-based P2P-transactions.

For most public blockchains, the P2P system's messaging infrastructure is facilitated through the use of public-key cryptography. In Bitcoin, the establishment of ownership is enabled by the interconnection of private and public keys, addresses, and digital signatures (Antonopoulos 2015). The public key is used to receive the native blockchain asset (e.g. Bitcoin) and the private key is used for signing transactions (Antonopoulos 2015). The public key is derived from the private key through the application of the hash algorithm SHA256 (for Bitcoin). Thus, public and private keys come in correspondent pairs and are usually stored in a digital wallet. These pairs of keys have a corresponding address, which is derived from the public key. So, via cryptographic methods, private key, public key and address are mathematically interconnected. While the address serves as a destination target for transactions, the public key serves for verifying the ownership of an address through their mathematical relation. As the public key is derived from the private key, the address is also related to the private key.

Digital signatures serve as a technical identifier of content and messages. Like a handwritten signature, a digital signature assigns an entity to a document or data. Digital signatures are created as a combination of a message's content (hashed) and a sender's private key, the letter of which encrypts the hash of the message. Consequently, a digital signature is unique for each differing piece of content or message. The verification by the receiver is facilitated through reversing the signing procedure using the public key of the sender, the signed document and the specified hash algorithm. The receiver hashes the signed document, thereby creating a hash, which can be compared to a hash created by decrypting the digital signature using the sender's public key. One hash comes from decrypting the sender's digital signature, the other one results from decrypting the message's content. If both hashes match, it guarantees for the receiver that the message or digital signature has not been tampered with during transit and it is verified that the sender is the author of the message. With regard to ownership attestation, Nakamoto specifies a bitcoin as being a chain of digital signatures allowing the payee to verify previous ownership (Nakamoto 2008).

The fundamental process of digital signature creation and verification is shown in Figure 2.11. After the hashing of a digital document, the hash is encrypted with the addition of the private key and thus a digitally signed document is created. For the purpose of verifying the signed document, the original document can now be hashed again, and the hash value can be compared with the encrypted signature previously anchored with the private key to verify that it is the original document.

In summary, a valid digital signature is necessary to conduct a transaction, as Bitcoin and other blockchain systems use digital signatures to prove ownership and a transaction requires the conductor to digitally sign and thereby authorize the transfer (Amati 2016). The digital signature can only be generated via a valid pair of digital keys (Antonopoulos 2015). It facilitates the process of verification of a transaction by other network participants and its inclusion in blocks. Together with the public key, the digital signature allows every network participant to validate transactions, ensuring that the transferred assets have been owned by the sender at the time of transfer (Antonopoulos 2015).

Mathematical conclusions

Encryption methods constitute an integral part of blockchain systems and are extensively applied. In the process of mining and creating pseudo-anonymous accounts for participants in the network, cryptographic means are applied in innovative ways. Their application enables the creation of a network that is in principle anonymous for

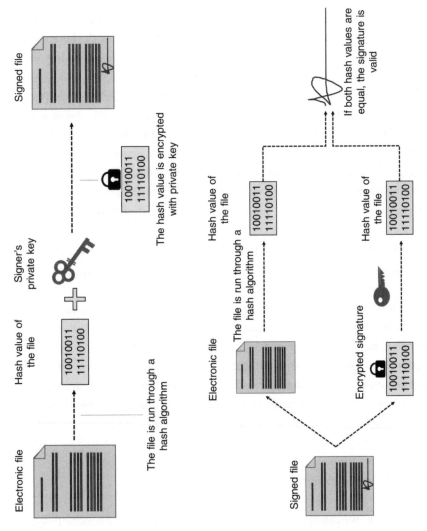

Figure 2.11 Simplified visualization of a digital signature creation and verification

participants, but transparent enough to allow all crucial information to be verified. In an interplay with economic elements, the technical and mathematical components enable the self-regulated and secure exchange of digital assets. Additionally, the incentivization to participate in mining makes the network security that accompanies the dedicated computing power a side effect of an economically incentivized competition.

In terms of public-key cryptography, it is important to understand that the applied mathematics are assembled in a highly sophisticated way, so as to ensure a trustworthy and verifiable open-source software construct. The public key is generated from the private key. Both together have a corresponding address, derived from the public key. A pair of keys is necessary to sign a transaction, which is a prerequisite for the transaction's verification and execution. With reference to Bitcoin, Antonopoulos (2015) describes digital keys as enabling Bitcoin's properties of decentralized trust and control, ownership attestation, and the cryptographic-proof security model.

In blockchain systems, messages are not directed from a sender of an asset to the intended receiver, but the message contains information to create a change of state in the distribution of the asset when it is validated. This message is directed to the whole network, propagated to neighbouring peers who conduct verification procedures and further propagate the message to their neighbours, theoretically, until the whole network has received the message. The message is directed to the network in order to be validated and included in a block, so the transfer eventually reaches a status of finality. The applied public key infrastructure thereby allows every receiver, propagator and validator to verify the contents and origin of the message.

2.3 ECONOMIC, POLITICAL AND SOCIAL COMPONENTS

P2P networks are about the cooperation of actors to achieve a synergy that utilizes participants' resources so that joint utilization is of greater utility than the sum of them individually (Antonopoulos 2015). Consequently, the participants have a certain responsibility to cooperate, in order to maintain the functionality of the network. A lack of cooperation puts the network's efficiency and its feasibility at risk. Obreiter and Nimis (2003) point out that P2P and similar systems "all build upon distributed systems of autonomous entities which need cooperation in order to achieve their local and global goal which leads to consumption of their possibly limited resources". This is also what it comes down to in blockchain systems.

In the following, we examine the incentive patterns used in P2P and blockchain systems, and how the interests of participants are aligned to ensure the liveliness of the network. "Liveliness" is a term from computer science, which describes a network that is capable of continuing its operations. It plays an important role in the development of distributed consensus, which we will describe in detail in the following section.

As all processing tasks in blockchain systems are decentralized and distributed across many actors, consensus mechanisms are implemented so that common, majority-led agreements about state changes are continuously attained. In blockchain systems consensus is established continuously and automatically. It presents a process of reconciliation and verification among many participants and can thus be regarded as an economic and social procedure for finding agreements.

In the realm of blockchain technology, "governance" describes how decisions are made that relate to how a network evolves, which technical measures are in line for discussion and implementation and how they are actually implemented. Moreover, blockchain systems differ in their structural organization for decision processes. They can be ruled by a minority of powerful players, the biggest stakeholders of a network, specific entities in the network, such as miners, a private company or a true majority of users, who vote on decisions. In this section, the most frequent democratic organizational structures of blockchain systems are explained. The governance of a public blockchain network can be regarded as being economically motivated or as being a social process. Both, economic and social motivations drive participants in the decision processes. The incentivization for running the network technically, the mechanisms of consensus for participants' collaboration and the structures for developing the network are interconnected. This section sheds light on how the components contribute to the complex construct of blockchain technology.

Consensus

Consensus in a blockchain network is continuously achieved in pre-defined intervals for the purpose of synchronization. Consensus algorithms are the mechanisms by which a system-wide agreement on the update of a system's state is achieved. Without a central entity, blockchains' consensus mechanisms administer a distributed consensus, which is supported by the majority of the network participants. Finding a distributed consensus is costly, because it requires coordination of many participants, but it reduces the dependencies and required trust in central entities to report an actual state, which can potentially be manipulated, censored or inaccessible due to downtimes or restrictions.

"Consensus mechanism" is a term from computer science and has been the subject of research for decades. It deals with the updating of a distributed shared state in a network through multiple replicas. The most common architecture of distributed consensus is the replicated state machine, a deterministic protocol designed to manage state transitions in networks of spatially separated computers. A shared state is distributed across a network via pre-defined state-transition rules and executed by the receiving network participants. That is to say that a replicated state machine acts as one but is actually replicated redundantly on every participating computer. State machine rules depict a technical frame for participants to produce the same output from executing the same input, which in turn creates a network-wide consensus on the state change that is replicated and distributed. Based on this consensus, the system transitions to the next state – a continuous set of processes. Participants communicate the results of their state changes to reconcile with connected nodes and eventually reach a final state (Baliga 2017).

Blockchain protocols are basically state-machine rules, whereas the current state of a blockchain can be described as the result of a continuous and chronological assembly of agreed state transitions of the distribution of a regarded digital asset or the digital representation of a physical asset. However, blockchain technology is more than just another distributed system. The most inventive element of blockchain technology to date is to be found in its base layer – the foundational consensus protocols. Blockchain's consensus protocols differentiate from traditional consensus mechanisms because they provide a practical solution to theoretical problems. To understand what differentiates blockchain from other systems, we need to dig a little deeper in the topic of distributed consensus and how it evolved.

The problem of finding consensus among a set of independent peers is a challenge, because correct processing needs to be ensured despite problems that are attributable to either (1) computer errors, (2) interrupted network reliability or (3) finding a global clock to determine the order of events. This means an algorithm needs to be resilient to the failures of nodes, to partitioning of the network, to message delays, to corrupted messages and to messages that are out of order (Baliga 2017). For a consensus to be achieved under disruptive circumstances, an algorithm must satisfy two basic conditions. There must be:

- Agreement: all truly acting nodes, or a majority of nodes, agree on a proposed state (output value);
- Termination: all truly acting nodes, or a majority of nodes, agree on a state.

Typically, a pre-selected participant proposes a state change to other network participants, who validate the proposition and declare a vote for that value to be valid or not. All network participants must now find the value, which is declared true by all or a majority of network participants. Communication among the nodes about the result of the voting prescribes a state transition through the distributed consensus mechanism.

This is a simplified and theoretical example, as in reality network environments can be synchronous or asynchronous. A synchronous environment is characterized by a certain predictability of its functionality: a message sent can be expected to be delivered within a certain timeframe. The internet, as we know it, is a rather asynchronous environment in which a sender has no guarantee that a message is delivered to its receiver. The internet infrastructure is subject to insecurity of functionality, centralized servers and latencies, which present threats to finding consensus as the processes of the consensus mechanisms might be interrupted or disturbed. For example, a node whose vote is required for finding the consensus does not receive a message or experiences an unexpected server downtime. Following this scenario, the condition of termination cannot be achieved, as all participants need to agree on some value.

In 1985, Fischer, Lynch and Patterson published a paper entitled "the impossibility of distributed consensus with one faulty process" (Fischer *et al.* 1985), also referred to as the "FLP impossibility", which became one of the most influential papers in the distributed computing research domain. The problem of finding consensus was known to be achievable in synchronous settings, for which processes are conducted simultaneously and iteratively. If a participant fails or crashes, the system can detect the faulty node by waiting one entire iteration. This way, this specific type of failure can be detected and dealt with by excluding them from further processes. In synchronous environments, consensus is predictable, because assumptions about the maximum time it takes for messages to be delivered are possible. This means, that in an iterative process, new participants can be selected to propose new transactions, voting about state transitions can be conducted and faulty participants skipped if they do not manage to respond within the pre-defined time slot. However, synchronous settings are somewhat controlled environments and therefore not practical, because distributed systems are distributed spatially and connected via the internet, and as we have learned, the internet is anything but a predictable and controlled environment.

In their paper, Fischer, Lynch and Patterson show that this kind of failure detection is not possible in asynchronous environments, in which time boundaries for a participant to conduct an operation or respond via a message are not defined. The system cannot distinguish between the failure of a node or a delay in operation due to the nature of an asynchronous environment (e.g. latency). Consequently, achieving the termination-condition of a consensus algorithm imposes a problem. The "FLP result" shows that a single faulty process makes it impossible to reach consensus in a deterministic asynchronous environment. The term "impossibility" in this case is quite strong. Basically, the asynchronous environment allows for delaying messages long enough, so that a bivalent configuration of the network state can result in a concluding bivalent configuration eventually resulting in an infinite loop of indecision, so that a univalent configuration becomes impossible, but still follows the protocol. They point out that no protocol can guarantee that a consensus might ever be reached. To work around this problem, research has modelled two basic possibilities: (1) despite modelling for asynchronous environments, assumptions for synchronous settings are still applied and (2) the condition of termination, that the participants need to agree on some value in the consensus process at all, is loosened to a result that is non-deterministic.

Consensus algorithm Paxos introduces time intervals for messages, thereby applying the synchronous assumption that a message will arrive. Put differently, Paxos's consensus mechanism is tranched in time intervals and if a node does not respond within the pre-defined interval, the process for the specific state transition starts all over again – without the non-responding node. This way, Paxos aims to achieve a guaranteed termination, enforcing the consensus through applying a synchronous assumption in an asynchronous environment. Algorithms like Paxos, Raft and other variants proposed in research literature tackle the problem of faultiness of specific nodes in the network, making the algorithm fault tolerant. In order for such algorithms to work adequately and ensure the safety of the network, the number of nodes needed is 2x+1, to be able to tolerate x faulty nodes. This way, a majority of non-faulty nodes in the network can keep up the progress and process further state transitions.

Up to this point in time, researchers have not found the solution of how distributed systems can be functional over the internet, while being open to every participant who wants to contribute. In particular, a problem has been identified to be the differentiation of faultiness of

participants. "Faultiness" is more than just nodes crashing or not re-
sponding due to network latencies. Another category of faults is a
"Byzantine" fault, which describes erratic behaviour by individual
nodes, who may have individual objectives that conflict with those of
other nodes. That is, nodes in the network are not controlled but may act
arbitrarily to pursue individual goals. This can result in a node sending
faulty or ambivalent messages, misleading other involved nodes or coordinating majorities to achieve consensus upon an individually desired
value, thereby changing the network's state in one's favour. The identification of this category of faults and their characterization was sum-
marized by Lamport *et al.* in 1982 in "The Byzantine Generals Problem"
(Lamport *et al.* 1982). This paper describes how computer systems
must handle malfunctioning components by presenting an analogy of
Byzantine military generals, who surround a hostile city with their ar-
mies and need to communicate with one another in order to agree on a
battle plan. Based on the assumption that some generals are traitors who
transmit false information, the paper discusses how consensus might be
achieved. As a solution, Lamport *et al.* (1982) determine consensus to
be obtained when less than one third of all nodes transmit false information to the network. In mathematical terms, Lamport *et al.* show that the
communication problem can be solved when the number of non-faulty
nodes outnumbers the number of faulty nodes by $3x+1$ with x being the
number of faulty nodes.

Consensus algorithms for open networks, in which arbitrary behaviour by individual nodes is possible, need to be capable of handling the
presence of faulty nodes (Byzantine fault tolerance) in order to ensure
the correctness and functionality of the system. However, the Byzantine
generals problem proposes a solution for synchronous settings only.
The desired achievement must be to create a consensus algorithm that
is practical and applicable in an asynchronous setting, while being tolerant towards Byzantine behaviour. For achieving this, Dwork, Lynch
and Stockmeyer (1988) proposed a model to find "consensus in the presence of partial synchrony". It basically means that the assumptions of
synchronous or asynchronous settings are neglected in favour of partial
synchronous settings, for which Dwork, Lynch and Stockmeyer show

that consensus is possible. They introduced a new assumption, the partial synchronism, and proposed to split the condition for correctness (agreement and termination conditions) into two, a safety and a liveliness condition. This adds up to three crucial properties, which consensus algorithms need to have:

- Safety: framed by the rules of the protocol, a network is considered safe when all non-faulty nodes produce the same output and the output is valid. This is referred to as the consistency of the shared state, an agreed transaction log despite both categorial faults.
- Liveliness: this property depicts a modified termination condition. While the termination condition requires the non-faulty nodes to agree on some output value, the liveliness property describes that a network needs to progress so that its functionality is ensured. The partial synchronism assumption is made for ensuring the liveliness condition, which in turn overcomes the FLP impossibility.
- Fault tolerance: for a network to continuously reach consensus on state transitions, the consensus algorithm needs to be able to handle faulty nodes that experience either technical failure or are Byzantine faulty.

The paper shows that consensus can satisfy the safety condition without applying the synchronism assumption. However, the proposed algorithms by Dwork, Lynch and Stockmeyer work on the assumption of a global time among the network participants through a "distributed clock". This is not practical for real applications and therefore it has not been widely implemented.

The practical Byzantine fault tolerance (PBFT) algorithm, proposed by Castro and Liskov (1999), presents a fault-tolerant algorithm that addresses the problems of previous algorithms. It is applicable in asynchronous settings and improved in terms of speed. That is, several improvements have been implemented, such as reducing computational efforts for message-verification schemes (public-key infrastructure) by replacing part with message-authentication codes (MAC), while reducing the overall number of messages required in the processes.

PBFT implements a scheme of primary nodes and secondary "backups", in which the secondary nodes conduct verification checks of the primary proposal and can collectively switch to another primary node if the primary node is found to be compromised (Baliga 2017). Regardless of the optimizations in PBFT, the algorithm still did not turn out to be practical enough for most real-world applications. However, PBFT circumvents the FLP impossibility by assuming synchronism for liveliness (not for the safety assumption) which presents another step towards satisfying both applicability in asynchronous environments while satisfying Byzantine fault tolerance.

Most blockchain networks do not differ much from the systems for which the previously described algorithms have been researched and developed. In fact, the same properties are required for blockchain protocols in order to find consensus in asynchronous environments: safety, liveliness and fault tolerance. The point with blockchain, and what makes Bitcoin inventive and special, is that a new approach has been found to overcome the FLP impossibility. Blockchain technology implements a consensus algorithm, which does not assume synchronism in asynchronous environments but changes the prerequisite of termination into non-termination. Creating a non-deterministic system has turned out to be a suitable choice when the distributed system was designed, because the nature of the state transition in Bitcoin combined with economic incentives and cryptographically enchained record-keeping eventually reduces the effect of state changes (new blocks) being non-deterministic to a negligible probability. In other words, a state transition in a blockchain system is not deterministic and technically violates the safety condition. But, the risk of non-termination is negligibly small and decreasing with increasing operational effort contributed to the system's liveliness (mining).

Basically, a transaction in a blockchain imposes a state transition, which can be regarded as final after a certain number of blocks have been added that build upon the block in which the transaction is included. The more blocks build upon the block in question, the smaller the probability becomes of that block being part of a conflicting transition log (a conflicting version of the blockchain or a "fork") and the probability decreases that the transaction can be manipulated or becomes invalid.

Consensus algorithms are always developed in restriction of trade-offs. The most suitable for blockchain was found to be an adjustment of the termination condition. Basically, the coordination operations of Nakamoto's consensus do not require every node in the network to participate, which would imply a quadric number of network connections (every node connects with every node). Instead, the findings of the consensus algorithm are probabilistic – nodes agree on the probability of the correctness of the value that results from the consensus processes. This paves the way for Bitcoin's and blockchains' scalability. Scalability here refers to a nearly unlimited number of users who can join the network. Thereby, an increase in users does not stress the system, but in fact, strengthens the network in terms of security.

Moreover, the mechanism for choosing a leader to propose a new block is not randomized but stems from a competition for solving a computational task, which we explained in the section on hash algorithms. Having achieved the desired outcome, a node becomes a proposer. Compared to the previously reviewed algorithmic consensus approaches, this is a rather complex and costly element. But it is innovative in this case, because through block rewards and transaction fees, a node is constantly incentivized to participate in the game of choosing a proposer of the next block. Nodes that participate become economic actors, as they input certain expenses in the form of computational power (CPU power) to eventually receive an economically utilizable outcome. The chance of becoming a proposer relates to the fractional CPU power that a node contributes in relation to the global CPU power contributed by all participating nodes. In case two nodes present correct values, conflicting blockchain extensions can occur. Such conflicts are addressed in the protocol, so that the network always builds upon the chain for which the most computational effort can be attributed (the longest chain). As long as a majority of nodes is controlled by non-faulty nodes, an attack of malicious actors for comprising the blockchain is prevented.

Proof-of-work (PoW) is the most widely known consensus algorithm, introduced by Bitcoin. PoW can be considered the most important invention underpinning Bitcoin (Antonopoulos & Wood 2018). As we have mentioned before, the PoW consensus mechanism is commonly referred to as "mining". This is a rather misleading term, as mining not only includes minting new bitcoins, but contributing computing power to the network, which secures the network and thereby the integrity of the blockchain. The real purpose of the PoW is "to secure the blockchain, while keeping control over the system decentralized and diffused across many participants as possible" (Antonopoulos & Wood 2018: 320). The incentivization of nodes through the pre-defined block reward and additional transaction fees from the transactions included in the blocks ensures the miners' incentivization. As miners face costs for conducting the required computations, they act economically. Miners act economically by being honest, as long as more than 50 per cent of the network's contributed CPU comes from honest miners. However, dishonest action requires unrealistic coordination of distributed CPUs and a collective attack on the rest of the participants.

The general task of miners taking part in the PoW algorithm is agreeing on who becomes the leader to propose a block. This is done through a mathematical task that all miners try to solve simultaneously using specialized hardware and software. The solution can only be guessed, which means that a process has to be conducted repeatedly to continuously generate results until a desired result is found by one miner. The difficulty of the task can be adjusted according to the CPU that is dedicated to the network in total, while the goal of the difficulty adjustment is to secure a new block production every ten minutes. In other words, the difficulty of the task is always adjusted for all participants to take an average of ten minutes to be solved.

The concept of proof-of-stake (PoS) basically formulates that consensus is reached based on a financial stake – those who have the highest interest (stake) in the honest continuation of the system are the ones to validate and process transactions (and blocks). PoS introduces a system of reward and punishment, by allowing participants in the network, who own a regarded blockchain's inherent cryptocurrency, to lock those into deposit using a special type of transaction. By locking their stake, they vote on a specific candidate block being valid. They are encouraged for being honest, because if they vote on a block, which is rejected by the majority of voters, they lose their stake. If a block turns out to be accepted by the majority, voters receive a proportional reward. In contrast to PoW, in which losses are extrinsic (costs of electricity), losses in PoS are intrinsic (losing cryptocurrency at stake; Antonopoulos & Wood 2018). PoS possibly offers various advantages in comparison to PoW, as the consensus is reached with less electricity, the danger of a 51 per cent attack can be decreased, and blocks can be found at a faster pace. Yet, correspondent to the possibility of advantages several obstacles like the so-called nothing-at-stake problem occur, in which validators do not have an incentive to act honestly (Buterin 2014a).

In order to use PBFT as the mechanism of consensus, the total number of nodes must be known, which makes this mechanism difficult to adopt for public blockchains. The underlying idea of PBFT is that a pre-defined amount of trusted actors sign transactions before they are broadcasted on the network. As an example, a permissioned, private ledger that consists of ten banks would require consistent block validations from at least seven out of ten banks in order to generate a new block. PBFT is used in permissioned, private blockchains.

Figure 2.12 provides an overview of consensus mechanisms that are applied in distributed networks. It shows that several concepts for such mechanisms exist. As an example, the concept of proof-of-importance (PoI) validation binds the level of importance of a user to the ability to verify transactions. Importance is defined by the number of total transactions that a participant has ever conducted. The underlying idea of PoI is that individuals who generate a high transaction volume are highly incentivized to act truthfully. Different types of consensus mechanisms can be combined in order to increase the amount of security granted: Peercoin is an example of a cryptocurrency that implements both PoS and PoW. The project Lisk implemented delegated PoS (dPoS) in which users vote on delegates and collectively decide who is the most reputable and trustworthy entity in the network. Once successfully elected, these delegates

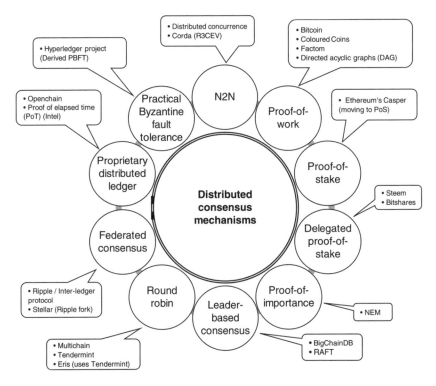

Figure 2.12 Distributed consensus mechanisms

Source: adapted from KPMG (2016: 4).

are in charge of validating new blocks and are compensated for their efforts.

Distributed consensus mechanisms stand at the heart of blockchains. New algorithms are being introduced and implemented constantly. It is essential to understand that each design choice for reaching consensus is accompanied by pros and cons that stem from trade-offs, such as scalability of network participants and validators versus transaction throughput. Deeply connected with the consensus algorithm is the question of how such decentralized systems can be governed and how technical improvements can be decided on. The next section unravels the processes of governance in decentralized systems.

Governance

Public blockchain systems strive for decentralization in order to form self-maintained and collectively governed networks of collaboration – it is about empowering users, while reducing individual and collective dependencies. Accordingly, governance structures that are implemented often have democratic characteristics and decision-management built in. Blockchain governance describes the ability of an ecosystem to adapt to changing environments and implement technical improvements. Moreover, governance relates to how applications that utilize blockchain as an infrastructure agree on decisions. In this section, we explore the knowledge of how blockchain systems are administered and the challenges associated with a distributed way of governing organizations. This is essential for understanding how blockchain systems can facilitate empowerment of individuals, which we explore in Chapter 3.

Governance in blockchain systems does not differ much from governance structures in IT. It is suitable to explain blockchain governance characteristics and challenges alongside the academic research on IT governance, whose structures have been extensively assessed academically (Brown & Grant 2005). Despite most of the former research focusing on dimensions and practices of how to invest in and apply IT in corporate environments, these concepts are transferable to decentralized organizations such as blockchain systems. The IT Governance Institute defines IT governance as "a structure of relationships and processes to control the enterprise in order to achieve the enterprise's goals by adding value while balancing risk versus return over IT and its processes". A more specific definition comes from Weill and Ross (2004: 2) focusing on the relationships and processes of control: IT governance is defined as "specifying the decision rights and accountability framework to encourage desirable behaviour in using IT". Weill and Ross's definition highlights three relevant dimensions: decision rights, accountability and incentives.

Decision rights either relate to decision-management rights or decision-control rights. Decision-management rights describe the capability to develop, propose and implement decisions while decision-control rights represent the competence to monitor decision-making processes and eventually initiate a ratification of a decision (Fama & Jensen 1983). Decision-control and decision-management rights should be separated to reduce the opportunities of self-monitoring and self-rewarding (Moldoveanu & Martin 2001).

Accountability refers to the allocation of responsibilities of the outcomes of implemented decisions and is linked to decision-control rights. Contracts and legal frameworks enact and enforce accountability. The accountability for decisions can be either institutionally or even technically enacted (Figure 2.13). Incentives are important in the realm of IT governance, because they enable the interests of agents, who make decisions, and principals, who delegate decisions, to be aligned (Jensen & Meckling 1976). That is, the owner of a company may have differing goals to the management employed. Incentive alignment in the form of pecuniary or non-pecuniary rewards ensures that agents act according to their mandate. More specifically in the IT realm, interests are aligned if users use the system consistently with the design objective it was intended for (Ba *et al.* 2001). Figure 2.13 visualizes an IT governance

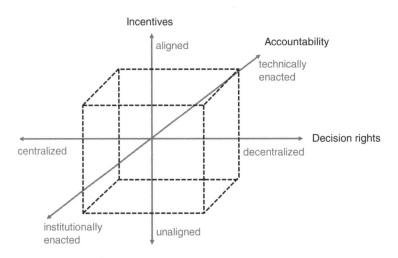

Figure 2.13 Extended IT governance framework

Source: adapted from Beck *et al.* (2018).

framework, including the dimensions of decision rights, accountability and incentives.

IT governance of blockchain systems at the infrastructure level must be differentiated from IT governance of applications, companies and projects which employ and build on these infrastructures. Numerous companies have created businesses and projects, whose business models or purpose involve the native cryptocurrency of their respective blockchain infrastructure or dedicated cryptographic tokens, which are tied to specific blockchains and serve specific functions in the project's software. In the following, such companies and projects are referred to as being part of the blockchain economy (in contrast to blockchain infrastructure projects). By owning cryptographic tokens of a project, owners have a stake in that company. In most cases, however, such a stake does not display any ownership rights in the respective company. Rather, tokens are speculative digital assets whose value increases when the demand for the developed product and, respectively, the token increases. As a result, owners of a specific cryptocurrency or token have some (speculative) stake in the system. The value of the stake they have depends on the properties assigned to that cryptocurrency or token by its creators. These might include (but are not limited to):

- Voting rights (token ownership allows for participation);
- Access to services (software usage involves regarded token, vouchers);
- Ownership in companies (equity) or assets (art, vehicles, commodities, real estate);
- Reputation (more tokens = higher reputation);
- Currency (means of payment).

The concept of tokens is a topic very much related to the funding of start-ups in initial coin offerings (ICO), which are events for selling tokens by projects that aim to develop or have developed a certain product in which the token plays an important role. We refer to this topic in detail in Chapter 4.

The governance of such decentralized blockchain applications differs from those of blockchain systems in so far as blockchain systems provide an infrastructure and those applications utilize that infrastructure. Both are confronted with other issues, accordingly. But, as most application-layer developments aim to create businesses and projects that are decentralized, which often involve the community-ownership of such organizations, they also share some similarities with regard to their governance. Other than pure for-profit companies, some application-layer projects, as well as most public blockchain infrastructure projects, most often aim to become decentralized in their management and ownership.

Decision rights can be concentrated and centralized in a single individual or group of individuals or be decentralized. The decentralization of decision rights in the context of corporate IT was discussed as far back as 1983. Decentralized decision-making is more expensive to monitor and creates overhead, as decision processes are redundantly implemented (King 1983). For public blockchain systems, the domain of IT governance is of utmost importance, because such systems are basically, or aim to become, community-owned organizations. Centralized decision processes would most probably not be acceptable to community members and run contrary to the motivation for blockchain technology's invention. Community members can have different roles and objectives, of course, some stakeholders are simply users while others are developers that build applications on top of a blockchain or maintain its infrastructure.

Across stakeholders, the goals might be similar, but the technical approaches to reach such goals can differ significantly. In the realm of blockchain technology, the best example relates to the extensive discussion about how technically to achieve an increase in the capabilities of the Bitcoin blockchain in terms of transaction throughput (scalability). The discussion ended up in a community split, including a "fork event", which describes the process of splitting the blockchain, so it grows in two directions in parallel. The result of the dispute was the creation of Bitcoin Cash as an alternative system to Bitcoin. Both extensions follow different principles (for increasing technical capabilities) manifested in the respective software that miners employ. Consequently, miners played a key role in resolving the dispute. Whichever software they run, they decide which part of the network they belong to, which technical solution they prefer and which blockchain they continue to work on. Such a decision process was democratic, as every individual miner receives one vote. But, referring to the computing power, these miners individually dedicate to securing the network and validating transactions, their vote is indirectly weighted, which is contrary to our understanding of democratic voting. Such an event is definitely not desirable in terms of security, because it creates two weakened systems out of one stronger system. On the other hand, it allows two different approaches to develop separately.

The distribution and characteristics of decision-management rights and decision-control rights differ across public blockchain infrastructure systems. In Bitcoin, every user can present Bitcoin improvement proposals (BIPs), which are a method for communicating ideas for discussion and eventual implementation (Figure 2.14). BIPs are documents that provide information about a new Bitcoin feature, its processes or environment, with a concise technical specification.[4] It is incumbent on the author of the proposal to generate consensus and support for their proposal. Before being submitted to the Bitcoin developer mailing list, it has to pass checks and finally be evaluated sophisticated enough to even be discussed.

The concept and roadmap for improvements for Bitcoin has been largely copied from Python's PEP-0001 (Python enhancement proposal), which ensures a standard workflow for proposing, discussing, modifying and implementing technical improvements to the original code. Ever since the first BIP in 2011, Bitcoin's code has been constantly

---

4. For more information see https://github.com/bitcoin/bips/blob/master/bip-0001.mediawiki (accessed 12 April 2020).

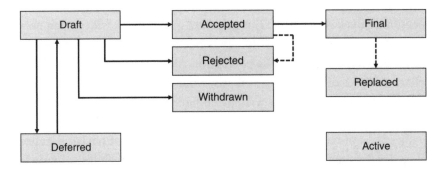

Figure 2.14 Possible paths of the status of Bitcoin improvement proposals

Source: adapted from Bitcoin Wiki (https://github.com/bitcoin/bips/blob/master/bip-0001.mediawiki, last accessed 12 April 2020).

modified using this workflow.[5] Other projects use similar workflows, such as Ethereum (Ethereum improvement proposal; EIP) and NEO (NEO enhancement proposal; NEP). On the one hand the governance of the organization through modifying its code is centrally administered; but, on the other hand, improvements to the code are peer-reviewed, extensively discussed and sophisticated. Moreover, everyone can potentially contribute. Following the workflow until the acceptance of a BIP and its reference implementation, some BIPs require miners to vote on their acceptance. The miners' votes and the software they employ, are partly transparent.[6] Acceptance requires the community to upgrade their software.

In any other company involved in the digital economy, accountability of governance decisions entails legal risks and obligations, which are most often associated with those stakeholders that control decision-making. The overall legal frameworks and regulations which affect the digital economy are, of course, also relevant for the blockchain

---

5. A list of implemented BIPs into Bitcoin's reference implementation Bitcoin Core can be viewed at: https://github.com/bitcoin/bitcoin/blob/master/doc/bips.md (accessed 12 April 2020).
6. See, for example, https://coin.dance/nodes (accessed 12 April 2020).

economy (Beck *et al.* 2018). This calls into question the widespread perception that blockchain technology is out of the reach of national and international legislation. This perception stems from the decentralized characteristics of blockchain systems, which often claim to be or aspire to be community-owned as well, having no single owner in the form of a company or an individual. Still, effectively regulating decentralized organizations of blockchain infrastructure systems is not trivial, because their legal status does not allow for assigning responsibilities towards national or international legislations.

Rather, blockchain systems indirectly and inherently delegate their legal risks and obligations to network participants (Beck *et al.* 2018), especially those who utilize the infrastructure for building applications on top of it. However, applications built on blockchain infrastructure often decentralize their organizations so as to make them community-owned as well. Consequently, accountability is assigned to those participants who make use of an infrastructure, build services on top of it whether through a privately owned profit-oriented company, a non-profit organization or a decentralized, user-managed technical organization. Users of a decentralized platform, which offer services, become economic players and their economic activity becomes subject to their local legislation. But, a crucial element of today's blockchain infrastructure is that it facilitates service provision and service requests in an anonymous fashion. Consequently, effective enforcement of regulation across anonymous service providers on decentralized platforms can pose a potential problem for governments' law enforcement. Service providers and users can choose to become a known identity and comply with their specific regulations or stay (pseudo) anonymous.

In the case of blockchain infrastructure systems, assigning accountability of measures affecting regulation is similarly complex. The general question of who can be made accountable for creating a decentralized financial system, which, for example, can be used for money-laundering activity remains unanswered to date. It is hard to imagine making blockchain developers accountable for providing an infrastructure, which is used by anonymous gambling application providers (who do not comply with gambling regulation, for example by not identifying players), which in turn is used by criminals to launder money. Gambling is a topic of special interest, because blockchain technology affects it in numerous ways, which we will explain in detail in Chapter 4. Moreover, it is hard to imagine that blockchain developers are accountable for democratically deciding on the technical implementation of an improvement proposal, which might conflict any existing regulation.

Blockchain infrastructure projects incentivize network participants to collaborate on a technical level to keep the network running (remember decentralizing processing tasks), whereas blockchain economy projects often decentralize existing platform approaches, and redistribute fees and value associated with such platforms to its users. Whereas a profit-driven company such as Uber generates fees for facilitating its matching platform, blockchain economy projects aim to diminish central ownership and incentivize users to use their platform by redistributing profits. In theory, platforms are established which are superior to centralized pendants through reduced operational and legal dependencies, fair and transparent fee structure and overall lower costs for users.

Incentive patterns

The topic of incentivization in public blockchain infrastructure systems relates to incentivization patterns in P2P systems. Because such infrastructures provide the base level of application-based user interaction, their incentivization schemes are analyzed more in-depth in this section. It is important to appreciate the bandwidth of incentivization schemes applied in blockchain systems, because it lays the foundation for evaluating systems' functionalities and vulnerabilities. The relevance of incentivization is high for blockchain systems, because they are collective efforts in which none of the individual participants is expected to be altruistic. Rather, participants are economic actors, which collectively form a construct of social relevance. Public blockchain networks reduce dependencies of individuals and lower the barriers for individuals' inclusion in economic and social exchange.

An incentive pattern comprises a set of abstract mechanisms for promoting cooperation. Cooperation can be deconstructed into its very basic elements, relating to entities with certain roles who conduct specific actions and reactions. A provider of a service and a consumer of a service have different roles in this very basic setting (see Figure 2.15). While the provider lets the consumer use the desired service, the consumer remunerates the provider giving an incentive for the provider to accurately and continuously provide his service. The remuneration compensates the provider for its resource consumption (Obreiter & Nimis 2003).

Traditional client–server architectures are characterized by an asymmetry in the participants' static roles and hierarchy. That is, the server is intrinsically made available to serve requests from clients, while any collaboration between different clients or between clients and providers that exceeds the basic communication of requests and concluding provision is not expected nor facilitated. The asymmetry in the setting of a requesting client and an authoritative provider results in static behavioural patterns. In contrast to that, P2P systems are characterized by equal status participants, who can have various roles in the network, switching from provider to clients at a time or serving both roles simultaneously. P2P systems often lack an authoritative entity, which could oversee and punish malicious behaviour of individuals or groups. Because the synergetic collaboration of participants in P2P networks is crucial for

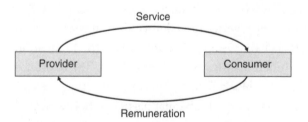

Figure 2.15 The terminology of elementary cooperation

Source: adapted from Obreiter & Nimis (2003: 90).

preserving its efficiency and feasibility, incentive mechanisms are an important means in decentralized network architectures for ensuring desired behaviours of the participants (Manzato & da Fonseca 2010). In other words, incentive mechanisms impose crucial design elements that ensure a network's performance and success through encouraging participants to cooperate.

As described, the feasibility of P2P networks is preserved by participants dedicating resources to the network. Such resources can be bandwidth, storage or computing power, which incur costs for the participants. By implementing incentivization schemes in P2P architectures, the relative costs and benefits of certain behavioural choices of participants can be influenced. Participants become economic actors, who face trade-offs, whose behaviour is expected to be rational and potentially can be forecasted, channelled or influenced.

In consequence, incentive mechanisms are designed to discourage uncooperative behaviour and allow for aligning and securing participants' interests. Incentive patterns can be numerous and consist of varying sets of abstract mechanisms for stimulating cooperation (Obreiter & Nimis 2003). Incentive patterns in P2P systems share general characteristics, referring to roles, remuneration, trust and scalability. Roles refer to the entities, which are part of the cooperation. An incentive pattern may encourage a provider to serve a consumer's request (asymmetric roles). However, in P2P systems the roles of the entities can be symmetric as a consumer might only be able consume a service, if they themself offer a service as well. They then take the role of the provider and requester simultaneously. Remuneration can be of different types and specific to the corresponding incentive pattern. It can have varying granularities, be intangible or tangible, like reputation or Bitcoin, be either transferable or stored. Trust is an important characteristic of incentive patterns, as it either constitutes an intangible incentive (reputation) or is a prerequisite for specific remuneration mechanisms. Trust can be required by the consumer towards the provider for executing the service and vice versa regarding the validity of the remuneration. In specific settings, the prerequisite for trust requires revealing an entity's identity. Another characteristic of incentive patterns is scalability. Scalability, in this context, refers to the capacity of the incentive pattern to remain efficient and effective as the number of participants increase. In a growing collective, it becomes increasingly challenging to communicate and ensure authenticity (Manzato & da Fonseca 2010).

Obreiter and Nimis (2003) propose a taxonomy of incentive patterns in P2P systems, which encompasses tangible as well as intangible patterns of remuneration (Figure 2.16). Again, the overarching goal of the incentive patterns is to foster cooperation among network participants in P2P systems.

As visualized in Figure 2.16, incentive patterns can be divided between trust-based patterns and trade-based patterns. Trust-based patterns refer to cooperation between provider and consumer on the basis of static or dynamic trust, without involving an explicit remuneration from the consumer for the service provider. Cooperation can be facilitated voluntarily by a provider, because both provider and consumer are part of a group which shares ideals (collective trust-based pattern). The collective pattern is characterized by participants' aligned interests about maintaining the feasibility and functionality of a network over

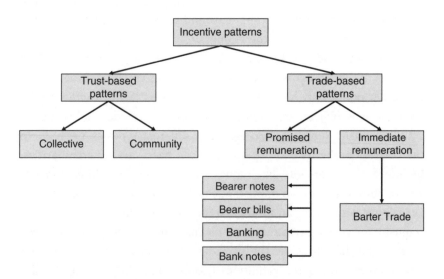

Figure 2.16 Taxonomy of incentive patterns

Source: adapted from Obreiter & Nimis (2003: 636).

individual interests. In contrast to all other incentive patterns presented in the following, the collective pattern does not encompass an explicit remuneration, such as reputation, monetary or service provision in return. In fact, gaining an individual advantage over others in the collective as a result of malicious behaviour, would weaken the whole collective. Collective incentive patterns in networks of trusted entities are less scalable compared to other patterns, because building the involved trust is expensive and time-intensive.

The service provider can also profit from an increasingly positive reputation by continuously providing services in the network, which is accounted for in a community trust-based pattern. In contrast to the collective pattern, individual interest in enhancing a reputation is the main driver for cooperation in these patterns. An entity with a certain reputation can expect to be able to enjoy cooperation with other providers. The involved trust towards the provider is dynamic, based on past behaviour and the availability of reputational information. In community patterns reputation is the remuneration of cooperation. However, both trust-based incentive patterns suffer from a lack of scalability. In a growing community of individual actors, the storage and availability of reputational information, defamation of good cooperators and false praise for non-cooperators impose challenges for the scaling of those patterns. Trust-based patterns are generally less scalable, as an increasing number of participants may not be compatible with a limited number of trusted cooperators, because trust needs to be earned.

In most blockchain systems, incentive patterns involve explicit remuneration for providers' cooperation. Referring to Figure 2.16, trade-based patterns include those categorized into promised remuneration patterns and immediate remuneration patterns. The barter trade pattern describes a simultaneous cooperation of providers. A provider's remuneration comes in enjoying a service at the same time as providing a service. This results in a situation in which non-cooperative providers are not able to enjoy services. The network participants' roles are symmetrical, which is only the case in the barter-trade pattern. In such incentivized networks, an increased provisional capability can be linked linearly to an increased capability of consumption. In other words, if a provider is capable of providing "their" goods extensively, they are in turn able to consume more. Advantages of this pattern are that it offers a comparably high scalability due to the direct linkage of cooperation and remuneration while diminishing the need for storage of remuneration and its related processes. Moreover, mutual trust between participants is not necessary. Shortcomings include the applicability of the incentive pattern only for specific products or services, so as to ensure that the remuneration is fair compared to the service provided (equivalence of transactions), as well as the technical requirement for participants to stay technically connected during the whole transaction. This pattern has mostly been applied in file-sharing networks (Obreiter & Nimis 2003).

In contrast to the barter-trade pattern, bond-based patterns involve payment from the consumer towards the provider. A bond thereby represents the debt of remuneration that results from the consumer's service usage. This enables a separation of cooperation and remuneration. A bearer note represents a promissory note from the consumer to the provider to cooperate in the future, while a bearer bill represents a promise to cooperate with the provider at a later point in time through an involved third party. Following this, the debtor and issuer of a note can be different entities (bearer bill) or the same entity (bearer note). Both patterns are limited in their scalability because they involve the need for trust to a certain extent. That is, it is costly to assess the trustworthiness of actors and issuers of promissory notes (Obreiter & Nimis 2003).

The so-called "banking pattern" presents a "bearer bills and notes" pattern, in which the promissory notes are more like checks – the debtor is a third party. Accounts at the third-party entity can be credited according to the checks, which allows actors to accumulate remuneration for future resource consumption. Such a third party, which takes on the role of a bank, can manage all accounts or a fraction of accounts. In this setting, the payment layer is outsourced to a third party, hence the moniker "banking pattern". Accordingly, cooperation for the service and remuneration are separated. In contrast to bearer bills and notes, the debtor is a reputable entity, which may increase the creditor's chances of actually receiving the promised remuneration. Because the service provision is decoupled from the remuneration and remuneration is ensured by a reputable third party, cooperation is more likely and less trust is required. Proving the authenticity of a service provider or assessing their trustworthiness from the perspective of a consumer is unnecessary as the third party becomes the debtor. A creditor does not need to assess the trustworthiness of a consumer only of the third party. Moreover, the creditor does not need to cultivate any reputation or prove their own trustworthiness.

The so-called "banknotes pattern" is similar to regular banking with banknotes issued by a third party (e.g. central bank) comparable to cash. Especially interesting are, of course, banknotes substitutes: digital assets that are inherent to the respective system (e.g. cryptocurrencies or tokenized shares). In computational systems, these substitutes must not be issued by a trusted third party. Rather, in the example of blockchain systems with inherent currencies or assets, means of payment are issued by a protocol. Here, assessing the trustworthiness of a third party is an assessment of the trustworthiness of a computational protocol. The banknotes pattern offers the most scalable incentive pattern because it does not involve dependencies on third parties (as in the banking pattern), it defers remuneration and service provision, it minimizes efforts for assessing the trustworthiness of actors and it allows for provider and consumer anonymity.

The incentive patterns implemented in most public blockchain systems are most similar to the banknotes pattern. In blockchain systems, banknotes are substituted by cryptographic tokens or coins as the medium of remuneration. The provided services encompass the verification and validation of transaction data, consensus participation and the propagation of transactions and blocks. Participants are not compensated for propagating transactions and blocks to their neighbouring peers. This pretty much presents a basic task for ensuring the functionality of the network and is performed by every individual client implementation automatically. The verification of transaction data and blocks are required for further propagating received messages, so such tasks are also not compensated. What is being compensated in public blockchain systems is the validation of transactions. In most public blockchain systems, participants can choose to become such a service provider (validator) by installing a certain type of software.

For service providers in blockchain networks, validating a transaction of a user relates to a banknotes pattern, as the user compensates the validator for including their transaction into a newly formed block by adding a fee. Some systems, however, employ a mechanism for finding out who is allowed to form a block. This adds additional computational efforts and electricity costs for service providers. To compensate service providers for their additional costs, a reward for forming a block is also included. This, of course, relates to systems with (temporarily) inflationary supply functions.

The processes of mining make the categorization of incentive patterns in blockchain systems non-trivial. As all service providers compete to form a block and consequently earn transaction fees and a block reward, the banknotes pattern is a probability-based remuneration. One might break down cooperation in blockchain systems into the processes between the formation of two concluding blocks and the actual block formation. Between the formation of blocks it is decided who out of all the service providers is allowed to provide the service and during a block formation the actual service provision and remuneration takes place. However, because the processes to decide which single service provider will provide their service are crucial for securing the network, it can be concluded that all service providers jointly serve the network by participating in the decision processes. They are not being compensated explicitly for this service, rather on an individual chance-based probability. The probability reflects the computing power dedicated by each individual service provider relative to the sum of computing power dedicated by all service providers.

As remuneration is based on probability and linked to the dedicated computing power, service providers can cooperate by jointly dedicating their combined resources. That is, by increasing their overall computing power, these service providers increase the chances of forming a block and being remunerated. As part of a so-called "mining pool", service providers with limited capacities increase the frequency of remuneration by coordinating their mining activity. Mining pool operators extract a fee from the acquired blocks' transaction fees and block rewards and distribute the rest among the pool members according to their dedicated computing power. In this case, the mining pool operator is an intermediary. In this separated setting, the incentive pattern is modified as the service provider is also a consumer of a service, which involves assessing the trustworthiness of the service provider. Assessing the trustworthiness of mining pool services is less costly, as the blockchain allows past payments and associated blocks to be reviewed and monitored.

Some public blockchain systems employ trust-based incentive patterns. Although associated with a lack of scalability for user growth scenarios, a community-selected and limited number of validators can be advantageous. By limiting the number of validators, the consensus process complexity is reduced, and more transactions can be processed in turn – a tendential centralization. In the context of incentive systems, this requires validators to earn reputation and users to assess the trustworthiness of these players. Moreover, for validator candidates it would be advantageous to reveal their identity. This kind of organizational structure is maintained by cryptocurrency system EOS. By implementing an inflationary supply function, validators get rewarded by the protocol creating new tokens out of thin air to remunerate these block-producing validators. EOS has no transaction fees for users at the cost of an inflationary supply and the centralization of operation.

Another incentive pattern is applied in the cryptocurrency system IOTA. In the IOTA system, submitting a transaction to the network requires the initiator to perform a verification and validation of two previous transactions. This creates a "multidimensional" blockchain, whose concept is called directed acyclic graph (DAG). IOTA's incentive pattern is comparable to the barter-trade pattern: rather than compensation in the form of tokens, the validation of a transaction (service provision) requires validation from two other users. Initiators of transactions thereby become service providers and consumers at the same time. In contrast to the barter-trade pattern, services are not consumed simultan-eously, but at different points in time, because the initiator of a transac-tion must wait for another initiator to validate his transaction, and so on.

The overarching incentive for forming consortium blockchains for private blockchain systems with restricted access and pre-selected par-ticipants is gaining efficiencies and enhancing collaboration, whether through transparency, processing speed or traceability. Such consortium blockchain approaches do not need to have complex processes installed for finding out who performs the processing tasks and gets remuner-ated. The processing tasks can be outsourced onto a jointly formed and financed entity of all participants or a third-party provider. Such set-tings differ significantly from maintaining the functionality in public networks of anonymous players, whose interests need to be aligned for collaboration.

Conclusions

Consensus mechanisms of public blockchain systems present a major invention in distributed computing. The mechanism initially employed in Bitcoin solves the puzzle for a Byzantine fault-tolerant algorithm which is applicable in asynchronous settings, by loosening the property of determinism. Transactions in a PoW-based blockchain environment do not experience true deterministic finality, but the probability of a transaction being revoked is ridiculously small and decreases signifi-cantly over time. By implementing incentive schemes for participants to act honestly and by implementing a costly consensus mechanism the al-leged weakness of non-determinism in the PoW is negligible. Although the non-determinism of PoW allows for several attack vectors, its high level of transparency, incentive schemes and the costs of attacks them-selves protect the system as it is.

Governance implementations can be differentiated across infra-structure projects and projects associated with the application-layer on top of these infrastructures. However, every project that aims to decentralize its platform or maintenance basically distributes decision rights (management versus control) and accountability across a net-work of participants. Decentralized decision rights introduce organiza-tional challenges and overhead, but create platforms, which can become community-owned and de-centrally administered while increasing the overall welfare in the ecosystem. Not only does this impose organiza-tional challenges to projects, but also in terms of regulation enforcement by governments. However, for most application-layer projects, as well as for a lot of blockchain infrastructure projects, a "benevolent dictator-ship" (Beck *et al.* 2018) is still necessary. That is, depending on the legal nature of the developing organization, there is a need initially to develop platforms of and on top of decentralized infrastructures. The claimed decentralization of decision rights and accountability is often only a fu-ture milestone on projects' development roadmaps.

The incentivization of participants in P2P systems has been subject to research for a long time. Public blockchains can be regarded as special kinds of P2P systems. That is why existing incentive mechanisms are identifiable in blockchain systems and applications. While for blockchain infrastructure projects incentives are implemented to encourage collab-oration among participants who lastly keep a network intact, blockchain projects on an application-layer incentivize the usage of their platforms through diminished platform fees and participation/voting rights for future developments.

In the previous chapter we have emphasized that a detailed de-scription of the technical, mathematical and economic foundations is important for understanding and assessing the value of blockchain sys-tems, why they were invented, how they can be applied and what im-pact they can have. As we have provided comprehensive descriptions of the components of the technology and their interplay, the following chapter explores some of the most important social impacts that the rise of blockchain technology has and could bring about in the future.

3

Potential and actual socio-economic impacts of blockchain

Data in qualitative and quantitative forms serve as a necessary foundation for social, political and economic life. Data can only unfold its true power if it is structured and put into a context to provide users with useful information for decision-making processes. By giving order to data, ledgers like blockchains, centralized databases or analogue registers allow ownership to be tracked – a function that is fundamental to the idea of property and modern society. Ledgers provide a record that coincides with the collective belief of a current state of affairs among members in a society. By introducing the idea of credit, ledgers became even more powerful by tracking who owes what to whom. Essentially, ledgers provide evidence for any change in the status quo and can be referred to during any dispute. Ledgers are fundamental to the organization of human affairs (Berg *et al.* 2018).

The oldest forms of ledgers date back to Babylonian temples. Ledger technologies have constantly evolved with double-entry bookkeeping and digital databases being the most notable breakthroughs of the modern era. Without them, modern economic and social infrastructure such as complex corporations, markets, administrations and governments could not exist. Not only do all organizations and institutions rely on storing and updating data in trustworthy ledgers, from the registration of births and deaths to home ownership, mortgages, credit cards and mobile phone contracts, our entire modern society is based on records and ledgers.

The maintenance of today's ledgers is regularly provided by the state and large corporations and all share one important characteristic:

centralization. There is one master ledger or database that is considered to hold the absolute truth. This provides enormous efficiency, since updates to the ledger only need to be conducted once in the central ledger by just one bookkeeper. At the same time, this bestows the central bookkeeper with enormous power, and it took centuries to develop political systems of checks and balances that prevent the wildest forms of misuse of this power. But even in modern democracies, the risk of exclusion is a constant threat to minorities. Apart from the risks that come with such power of central authority, centralized ledgers are inherently fragile, and the record can still be lost. There is also an increased danger of electronically held data being inaccessible, for example, by temporary power outages or hackers that encrypt a ledger and demand a ransom to decrypt it. The database could also be manipulated either through unauthorized access or corrupt gatekeepers or bookkeepers. In addition, large centrally controlled ledgers increase the likelihood of a seizure or hostile takeover. Blockchain, as a special type of DLT, promises to remove these risks by providing a way to keep and update a decentralized ledger electronically. While it remains an open question whether blockchain technology can indeed deliver on this promise – at least not at the expense of exorbitant inefficiencies or other risks – we focus in this chapter on the socio-economic effects decentralized ledgers already have, and on the potential they can have in the future.

DLTs are governance technologies that open new ways in which people can connect to information that were previously effectively unavailable in traditional ledger technologies. While pseudonymous transactions are a key feature of blockchain and DLT, one of their main innovations is the capacity to track transactions within decentralized, public databases that no one can be excluded from and that prevent counterfeits and fraud. Chaum had anticipated in 1985 that decentralized applications would offer a solution to problems of mass surveillance and democratic governance (Chaum 1985).

A core element of the socially disruptive power of most blockchains are the tokens that depict an initial state of allocation and can be transferred without a central authority to reflect an updated status of allocation. Tokens connect existing records in public or private ledgers with corresponding entries as tokens in a blockchain. Token applications can represent passports, birth or death certificates, vehicle registrations, or property records to credit ratings or biometric information among many others. This bridging from existing centralized records to newly created decentralized records allows to run redundant ledgers and thus could function as an additional layer of security for centralized ledgers. But it would also allow a smoother transition from a centralized to a decentralized ledger. In addition to the manual creation or transfers of tokens, smart contracts facilitate the automated transfer of tokens in accordance with predetermined rules. For example, distributed autonomous organizations' voting processes and ownership rights could be tokenized with smart contracts defining the rules that are automatically enforced and accompany with these rights.

A common narrative among crypto and blockchain enthusiasts is that blockchain-based tokens and smart contracts can radically redefine social and economic life. Such narratives play an important role in the politics and regulation of new technologies (Reijers & Coeckelbergh 2018) and influence how others perceive a technology and how it evolves. It is a recursive process in which narratives influence a technology and its adoption over time with changes again being reflected in the reinforcement of such narratives. Narratives thus not only shape how technologies are understood but also the development of the technology itself.

In the next section we provide an overview of the perceived and actual use of cryptocurrencies based on a survey of internet users. We then turn to more general and theoretical discussions on how DLTs can shape our society and discuss the potential for replacing intermediaries with a protocol. This is often claimed to reduce transaction costs considerably and bring huge efficiency gains for the economy. At the same time, replacing existing intermediaries comes with risks, especially when the transition is not a smooth process. There is a danger that existing intermediaries will resist the move or that people could be left behind, because they are digitally excluded. This illustration is followed by a discussion of censorship resistance, privacy and the effects of non-public but still verifiable information that are possibly provided through DLT.

Following this, the potential impact on property is considered and we explore the new markets and marketplaces that DLT could tap into and how this might reshape current markets and economies. The chapter concludes with a discussion of the cessation from current forms of centrally recorded social and economic life and the migration to decentralized alternatives that are not governed by central authorities. In sum the chapter works through the issues of decentralization, dis-intermediation, sovereignty and censorship resistance.

3.1 CRYPTO KNOWLEDGE AND CRYPTO USAGE

Blockchain-based cryptocurrencies have been in existence for ten years. Yet fundamental research gaps persist with regard to how they are perceived and used by the population. There is little research available into fundamental questions about the frequency of use, the composition of user groups, and the motivation to buy cryptocurrency. Public opinion still relies heavily on anecdotal evidence and guesstimates, leading to the perception of cryptocurrencies being a marginal phenomenon among some cypherpunks or that their only real-world application is for crime.

Postbank (2018) conducted one of the few representative surveys among 3,100 respondents, representative of the German population. While only 4 per cent of the respondents assigned themselves as having a "very good" and 16 per cent as having a "good" knowledge level, the majority counts itself less knowledgeable – 39 per cent stating "less good" and 41 per cent "poor" knowledge. Referring to digital natives (18–34 year olds), 29 per cent claimed to have a "very good" or "good" knowledge of blockchain. Another representative survey comes from BearingPoint (2018) among 2,020 German internet users, which found that 6 per cent actively use cryptocurrencies and are well educated about the topic, while 43 per cent have heard about cryptocurrencies, but have a limited knowledge, and 20 per cent do not know anything about cryptocurrencies at all. Gold IRA Guide (2019) conducted a survey among 1,000 US retirees. 32.9 per cent of the respondents had never heard of Bitcoin, whereas 56.7 per cent were aware of Bitcoin but did not consider it as an investment; and 2.7 per cent of the respondents owned Bitcoin.

According to Bitkom Research (2019), who conducted a representative telephone survey among 1,004 Germans over 16 years of age, 68 per cent have heard or read about cryptocurrencies, 56 per cent recognize that cryptocurrencies can speed up payment processes online, and 51 per cent are aware of cryptocurrencies' potentials to make transfers of money cheaper.

ING (2018) conducted the largest but non-representative survey among 14,828 respondents, aged 18 and above, in 15 countries, asking for the awareness of cryptocurrencies and ownership, including several European countries, Turkey, the United States and Australia. The awareness of cryptocurrencies among the respondents ranges from 38 per cent in Belgium to 79 per cent in Austria – in 11 out of 13 European countries, the majority of respondents had heard of cryptocurrencies. The authors identify a trend towards a higher ownership share among countries with lower income per capita.

These studies still leave a wide gap in socio-economic research, which the authors of this book aim to fill at the Blockchain Research Lab where they conducted a survey among 3,864 respondents, representative of the German internet population, to find out about mainstream awareness of cryptocurrencies and their state of adoption. Germany, as the largest European economy and most populous country, is a good example of a typical Western developed country; however, some caution is needed when it comes to generalizing these results to other Western countries. A common perception of cryptocurrencies holds that their use requires technical knowledge, and only the tech-savvy can understand how they work, their complexity being beyond most people's understanding. The survey was aimed at finding out who knows about cryptocurrencies and who owns them, especially with regard to age, gender, income and education.

According to the survey, 87 per cent of the population know about cryptocurrencies; 18 per cent of all adult internet users in Germany either currently own cryptocurrencies (9.2 per cent) or have owned some in the past (9.1 per cent).[1] Bitcoin leads its competitors by a long way in terms of usage, both among cryptocurrency users and among all respondents, and in terms of awareness: 83 per cent of respondents have heard of Bitcoin, and more than 80 per cent of all crypto users own Bitcoin. The rate of Bitcoin ownership among the sample stands at 7.5 per cent. Bitcoin Cash takes second place in terms of familiarity, followed by Ethereum and Litecoin. In terms of ownership, Ethereum is the second most popular cryptocurrency.

The diversity of cryptocurrencies is reflected in the fact that 54.7 per cent of the sample know cryptocurrencies other than Bitcoin, Bitcoin Cash, Ethereum, Litecoin, DASH and Ripple; 40.6 per cent of cryptocurrency users also possess these coins (Figure 3.1).

More than half of the respondents who currently hold or have in the past held cryptocurrency first acquired it between 2017 and 2019, which reflects the recent exponential growth in the industry. Still, quite a few have been active for a much longer period, stretching all the way back to 2009. Those who bought or mined early – in which case we are talking almost exclusively about Bitcoin – have likely enjoyed substantial gains, if they held on to their cryptocurrency long enough. This is evident if cryptocurrency adoption is plotted over time alongside the quarterly average Bitcoin price (Figure 3.2).

Motivational factors for using cryptocurrencies include making payments, speculation, value retention, criminal purposes, access to services, or start-up funding. In addition, respondents mention that ideology plays a strong role in their decision to own cryptocurrency. The cryptocurrency owners among the respondents were asked to indicate – on a scale from

---

1. The survey is representative of the general population in terms of age and gender, making the database much stronger compared to random surveys. The sample is not entirely representative in regard to other variables like, for example, education, a typical shortcoming of all surveys. This survey was conducted as an online panel and only comprises those who were willing to join and able to participate in a panel. Surveys in general suffer from similar limitations. For example, telephone surveys also have the bias that they require respondents not only to own a phone but also to accept an unknown caller and to have the time and interest to then answer the questions.

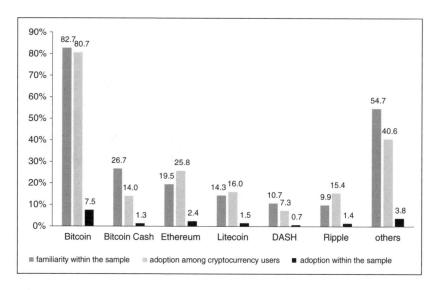

Figure 3.1 Familiarity and usage of cryptocurrencies

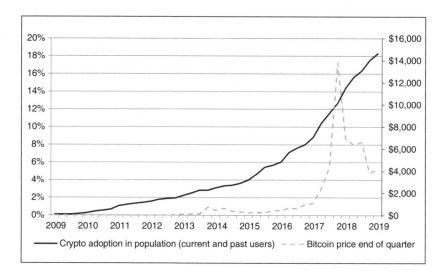

Figure 3.2 Cryptocurrency adoption in percentage of population versus Bitcoin price over time

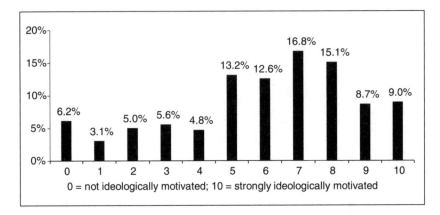

Figure 3.3 The ideological motivation for owning cryptocurrencies

0 (not ideologically motivated) to 10 (strongly ideologically motivated) – to what extent their holding of cryptocurrency is ideologically motivated (Figure 3.3) and 62 per cent of them stated their motivation was "predominantly ideological" (6 or above on the scale). It is unclear, however, what the specific ideological motivation of a particular user is. These can include political, personal, financial and other aspects and can arguably be heterogeneous across users. It would thus be interesting, and presents an important field for future research, to investigate the underlying ideologies for owning and using cryptocurrency in detail.

Current and past crypto-users are on average markedly younger than those who have never owned cryptocurrency (39 versus 48.5 years). They are also much more likely to be male (68.2 per cent versus 47.0 per cent). Cryptocurrency owners, past or present, have a higher education than non-users. A greater share of them has a university degree or even a PhD compared to non-owners, and fewer have completed none or only the lowest level of secondary education.

If a score is attached to each category of educational achievement, from 1 for "no secondary education certificate" to 5 for "PhD", with vocational and commercial training arbitrarily rated the same as "A-level equivalent", and each score is multiplied with the percentage of respondents who belong to each category, then those who own or have owned cryptocurrency are associated with a weighted average score of 3.21, as compared to 3.03 for non-owners (see Table 3.1).

Table 3.1 Cryptocurrency ownership in relation to educational status

Educational achievement	Score	Have you ever owned cryptocurrency?	
		Yes	No
No secondary education	1	0.6%	0.8%
GCSE equivalent	2	15.8%	22.2%
A-level equivalent	3	20.2%	14.5%
Vocational training	3	9.9%	15.0%
Commercial training	3	18.1%	22.7%
Higher-education degree	4	33.5%	23.3%
PhD	5	2.0%	1.6%
Average score		3.21	3.03

Cryptocurrency owners also differ from the non-owners with respect to their personal income – the former are markedly better off. Although this question only provided a choice of income brackets as answer options, it is possible to calculate a weighted average income for each group. Cryptocurrency owners enjoy an average net monthly household income of about €2,700, whereas the non-owners earn only about €2,000 (Table 3.2).

It is worth mentioning that there was a generally high level of awareness and a surprisingly widespread ownership of cryptocurrencies among the respondents. Both are indicative of cryptocurrencies being a phenomenon that persists not just among a few tech-savvy internet geeks but that it has increased in popularity and continues to grow. Still, with more than two thirds of all crypto owners being male, it is not uniformly adopted. Apart from the large gender gap the numbers also suggest that there is a "digital gap" leaving less educated people behind. There are clear ramifications for social inequality that should be of concern for regulators and society in general.

Table 3.2 Cryptocurrency ownership in relation to household income

Net monthly household income	Have you ever owned cryptocurrency?	
	Yes	No
Below €500	2.7%	6.7%
€500–€999	6.5%	12.5%
€1,000–€1,499	13.6%	17.6%
€1,500–€1,999	14.7%	16.4%
€2,000–€2,999	26.6%	21.5%
€3,000–€4,999	25.4%	15.3%
€5,000+	7.5%	3.6%
Average	€2,700	€2,000

In Germany cryptocurrencies are already widely adopted, even more than direct stock ownership. While it is unclear whether adoption rates are similarly high in other Western countries, the results still show that cryptocurrencies are neither a marginal nor a transitory phenomenon. The landscape of cryptocurrencies is expected to change over the coming years; it seems very unlikely that they will simply vanish. More in-depth research and monitoring by government and business is clearly required.

3.2 PERCEIVED AND ACTUAL USE OF CRYPTOCURRENCIES

So far, it is not clear how awareness about cryptocurrencies was developed in the general population. The prevailing attitude of each respondent towards cryptocurrencies may have been influenced by their sources of information. If cryptocurrencies are introduced by friends or co-workers, rather than through media coverage, an individual's response and perception about their trustworthiness will likely differ. Increased media coverage of cryptocurrencies in 2017 during a phase of massive price volatility, for example, influenced perception in our survey group.

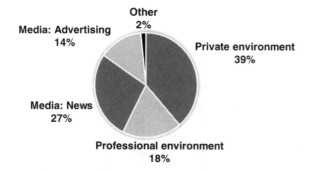

Figure 3.4 How respondents have had first contact with cryptocurrencies

In fact the majority of respondents were introduced to cryptocurrencies through personal contacts in their private and professional environment. Furthermore, 27 per cent of the respondents first became aware of cryptocurrencies through the news and 14 per cent through advertising (Figure 3.4). Given the importance of word-of-mouth in the transmission of information between peers or colleagues, the importance of the reputation of cryptocurrencies within the respective circle of acquaintances is of direct relevance.

Respondents were also asked "Do you perceive cryptocurrencies as trustworthy?" – 0 represents "not at all trustworthy" and 10 represents a "very high trustworthiness". "Trustworthiness" was deliberately not clarified and did not specify whether it included the underlying blockchain technology, market prices or relations to regulatory protection. The aim was to obtain a general index of attitude towards cryptocurrencies, rather than to provide a complete breakdown of all specific elements of trust that are involved with cryptocurrencies.

Scores for trustworthiness tended to be low with 75.3 per cent scoring less than 5 out of 10 and only 24.6 per cent scoring higher than 5 (6–10). Consequently, we can conclude that there remains a certain amount of scepticism and reservation among the internet population (Figure 3.5).

To delve into the question of trust towards cryptocurrencies, we divided the sample into three distinct groups with different self-assigned levels of knowledge about cryptocurrencies. Moreover, we divided the

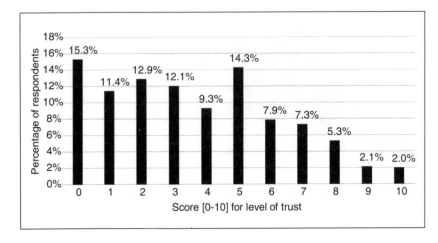

Figure 3.5 The level of trust in cryptocurrencies

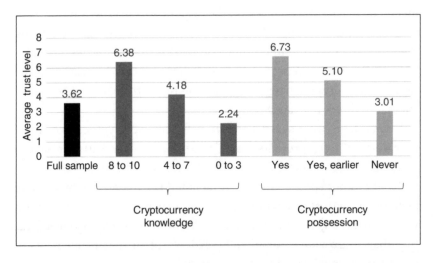

Figure 3.6 Average level of trust in cryptocurrencies for selected samples

sample into the three groups of current and former cryptocurrency owners, as well as individuals who had never owned cryptocurrencies.

Figure 3.6 shows the average scores for the level of trust in cryptocurrencies across the different samples. Unsurprisingly, levels of trust are higher amongst those with experience of cryptocurrencies than those who have less experience.

Given the strong positive effects not only of cryptocurrency owner-ship but also of knowledge on the trustworthiness scores, we tested for correlations between crypto knowledge, crypto ownership, and trust in cryptocurrencies. As the above results suggest, we found a positive correl-ation of knowledge and level of trust in cryptocurrencies (0.57). However, there are distinct differences among the subsamples. While there are posi-tive correlations of the level of trust in cryptocurrencies with respondents who currently own (0.40) or have formerly owned (0.19) cryptocurrencies, there is a negative correlation with respondents who have never owned cryptocurrencies (–0.44). The more interesting correlation we find is be-tween knowledge about cryptocurrencies and crypto possession: We find positive correlations with current (0.41) and, to a lesser extent, former (0.26) cryptocurrency owners, while a negative correlation is found with respondents who have never owned cryptocurrency (–0.50). All correl-ations are statistically significant (Table 3.3).

Overall, the level of trust towards cryptocurrencies is relatively weak. Trust might grow in the coming years with an increasing number of users. Unless there is a major upheaval, or revelations of illegal activ-ities via cryptocurrencies, confidence is likely to increase as the propor-tion of people using or having used cryptocurrencies grows. Moreover, as awareness and understanding of blockchain technology grows, the level of trust is also likely to increase. This process could be fuelled by a growing momentum in the use of cryptocurrencies.

Table 3.3 Correlations between cryptocurrency knowledge, ownership and trust

Item	Level of trust	Knowledge
Knowledge	0.5684*	–
Current owner	0.3986*	0.4081*
Former owner	0.1875*	0.2582*
Non-owner	–0.4419*	–0.4973*

*Statistically significant at the 1 per cent level.

A key indicator in terms of adoption is the actual usage of cryptocurrencies. We asked respondents how they used cryptocurrencies and contrast those results with the uses that respondents subjectively assume to be most relevant for cryptocurrencies. In terms of perceived purposes for the use of cryptocurrencies, there were differences in individuals who currently own cryptocurrencies, those who have previously owned some, and those who have never owned a cryptocurrency before. Asking for respondents' individual estimations on what they subjectively think cryptocurrencies are generally used for, we gather another indicator for attitudes and perceptions. It should be noted that these are merely assumptions of what respondents believe other people use cryptocurrencies for. We contrast this information with a question to current users of cryptocurrencies about how they actually utilize their currency.

The three most frequent perceived uses are short-term speculation, crime and the disguise of activities. Participation in elections and voting (current owner: 4.7; former owner: 4.4; never owned: 3.5) is given the lowest importance by all three groups of respondents followed by corporate and start-up financing (4.0; 5.2; 5.3). There is also a trend for current owners to estimate the importance of the different uses higher than those who had never owned cryptocurrencies. An interesting finding is the difference in the answers of the groups. These show a bias of either non-owners underestimating the use of cryptocurrencies for legitimate usage or owners overestimating these (Figure 3.7).

To compare the perceived usage, we asked current cryptocurrency owners how often they actually used cryptocurrencies for specific reasons. The frequency of use is a proxy for the importance of the respective use. Interestingly, the anticipated uses for cryptocurrencies differ significantly from the actual usage (Figure 3.8). For the respondents of the representative survey, long-term investment is used by far the most (3.5 days per month), followed by access to services (2.8 days), for example, dapps or services in the respective cryptocurrency's ecosystem. Moreover, cryptocurrencies are used for payment transactions (2.7 days), short-term speculation (2.5 days) and to disguise activities (2.5 days). By contrast, crime (1.6 days) and the participation in elections and votes (1.9 days) play the least important roles. We should perhaps

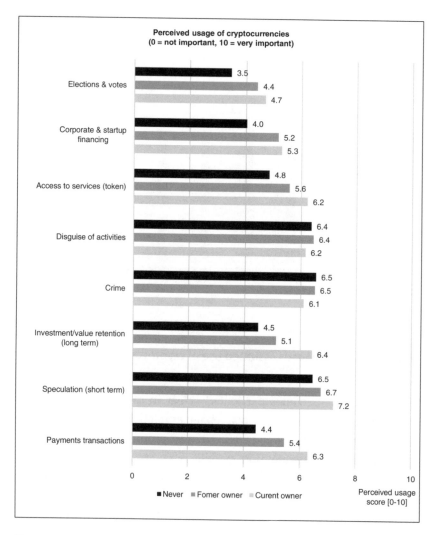

Figure 3.7 Perceived usage of cryptocurrencies

not be surprised that crime is mentioned least often given that even in an anonymous online questionnaire such activities are not readily admitted, so this result needs to be interpreted carefully.

The comparison of the actual use (represented by the average number of days per month and the assumed use (represented by a score of 0 to 10) of cryptocurrencies reveals clear discrepancies between these

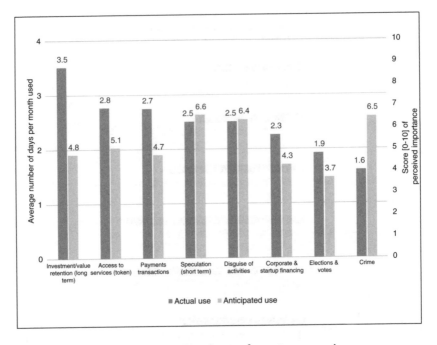

Figure 3.8 Actual versus assumed use of cryptocurrencies

two values. This becomes particularly clear in the case of crime and short-term speculation. These discrepancies might be attributable to the fact that these uses have been featured most prominently in the media.

These results indicate that people who are more familiar with cryptocurrencies consider potential risks to be lower, they actually have a deeper insight into what is going on around cryptocurrencies, but also they have fewer reservations. It could therefore be argued that a misconception exists about what cryptocurrencies are used for in the eyes of the general public. To understand why this gap exists, it is helpful to leave the idea of one "public" but instead consider that there can be more than one "public" that engage in different dialogues and controversies as is suggested by Linda Monsees who introduces the notion of "publicness" in her book on crypto politics (Monsees 2019). It remains to be seen, how these dialogues and controversies evolve in the future with further adoption, knowledge, education, and objective research.

3.3 DIS-INTERMEDIATION, LOCALIZATION AND INDIVIDUALIZATION

Imagine the following situation: Bob wants to buy a painting from Alice. They are located in different countries and cannot exchange the money for the painting in person. Bob does not want to send the money first and simply trust that Alice sends the painting. Alice, on the other hand, does not want to ship the painting first and trust that Bob sends the money after. Luckily, they both know Greg, a mutually trusted friend. So they decide that Bob sends the money to Greg, who then informs Alice that she can now ship the painting. Once Bob confirms the receipt of the painting, Greg sends the money to Alice. Greg is the intermediary without whom the transaction would not have been possible. Intermediaries are trusted parties that facilitate transactions between parties that otherwise would not interact with each other, for example, because they distrust each other (or, at least, not 100 per cent trust each other) or they do not have the technical means to communicate with each other, or simply not even know that the other side even exists.

Consider in our example that Bob values the painting of Alice at $1,000 while Alice values it at $600. They agree on a price of $800 and agree to share Greg's commission fee of $100 equally. Both Bob and Alice are then $150 better off compared to before the transaction. And if we count in Greg's bonus, the total added value – or what economists call a surplus – is $400.[2] All the transactions that become possible through intermediaries create huge benefits to society, because it makes everybody better off. Intermediaries consequently play a very important role in today's society and economy, and the business model of many of the

---

2. It could be argued that Greg's activity involved costs for him, for example, in form of time or work. This, as well as all other transactions costs, like shipping costs for the painting, need to be deducted to arrive at the net surplus. If the remaining surplus of a transaction is small but it also involves external costs that none of the involved parties has to directly cover – for example pollution caused by transportation – the net surplus could even become negative. All these specifics are important in detailed economic considerations, but we leave them aside for simplicity in explaining the role of an intermediary.

largest corporations, especially in finance, is to provide intermediary services.

One important narrative of blockchain is that it could facilitate the dis-intermediation of the economy and our society: trusted middlemen would be removed or replaced. But given the important role of inter- mediaries: why should this be beneficial? The answer is simply that such a dis-intermediation would not prevent transactions or their surplus, but simply replace existing intermediaries with a protocol promising that this comes at much lower transaction costs for the exchanging parties. If this is true, many transactions that currently are simply un- economical due to transaction costs could take place and create a huge economic boost. The costs of doing business could be reduced in general and new markets could evolve.

On the other hand, dis-intermediation could have adverse effects for the current middlemen, the institutions and their employees. For ex- ample, once central banks decide to issue money directly on a blockchain, people can hold money not only in cash and in a bank but also directly with the central bank. In such a system, payment processing could be- come a public good and intermediaries like credit card or e-wallet pro- viders would become less important or even obsolete. This would lead to a higher degree of transparency in payments that, in turn, could pre- vent tax evasion and money laundering. We will expand the topic of central-bank issued digital currency in Chapter 4. However, the reduc- tion in the importance of banks has ramifications that might lead to a financial crisis or bank runs. As with every new technology, the biggest changes are likely to stem from the disruptions caused by the transition to a new organization of society.

A shift from intermediaries that are people or directly controlled by people to protocols that do not allow human intervention, or only in very rare cases, transfers power back from the intermediaries to the acting entities – be they individuals, groups or organizations. Such power could be very positive in some circumstances, for example, when it allows for greater localization and individualization (which we explore in the following section). However, power cannot be shifted without re- sponsibility. If you forget your bank account password, you can simply go to the bank, prove your identity and be granted access to your account again. If someone loses access to their private keys in a blockchain-based environment, there is no one to turn to and accounts and stored assets are lost forever. While there are safeguards against such losses, these have to be put in place with precautions. Blockchain-based protocols require a considerable amount of technological know-how and so are not yet in a state where it would be reasonable to shift the responsibilities to the general population. Whether the technology will improve, in a way that the burden of responsibility shrinks significantly, remains to be seen. However, that does not mean that blockchain-based protocols cannot and should not act as intermediaries before then. They work perfectly well in areas where an intermediary has not existed before or as a redundant option for settings in which centralized intermediaries do exist. At the moment, however, it is premature to call for a replacement of centralized intermediaries.

But imagine a situation in which blockchain technology has evolved to a degree that makes it feasible to replace at least some centralized intermediaries with a blockchain or a smart contract, the traditional intermediaries are at risk of losing their power and their very reason to exist. We might expect them to try to keep their role in society and fight against such change. History provides many examples of technological development causing drastic social and economic changes, for example, the invention of spinning machines or steam engines in the industrial revolution.

If intermediaries were to be replaced by decentralized intermediaries, the role of the government in these spheres could change dramatically. It might start with decentralizing the registry for vehicles or companies before moving into the major roles like providing certificates for births, deaths, marriages, or the real-estate registry. Governments' roles would focus on providing a safe environment for the protocols that take over roles as intermediaries, providing infrastructure in the form of nodes and mining to prevent them from being corrupted. While counterfeiting is nearly impossible within blockchains, so long as the network is not corrupted, the transition between the physical world (or also digital but centralized databases) and the blockchain is the point at which the blockchain is most vulnerable to manipulation. Hence, it would be critical for the state to provide trustworthy oracles (entities bridging the physical and the digital space). So even in the event of powerful blockchain-based solutions, the state would continue to play an important and evolving role.

In the scenario in which decentralized protocols have taken over the role of some currently centralized intermediaries, it is not just the role of the state but society itself that will change. With the rising importance of autonomous machines, like self-driving cars, but also blockchain-based intermediaries, more and more social interactions will happen between humans and machines as well as between machines and machines. While this does not mean a lack or loss of human control – such interactions are not social in a human-centred way – the integration of non-human actors into our daily lives will change the inner workings of society. While we can speculate what such changes will actually look like, traditional human-oriented social theories would need to be adapted to understand these new phenomena.

Dis-intermediation also provides opportunities for a more localized and individualized society. Current centralized intermediaries tend to be very large to gain economies of scale. If these intermediaries become smaller or even cease to exist, localized markets potentially lose some of their current competitive disadvantages and, in turn, could flourish. This is further enhanced by the power (and responsibility) that is shifted towards individuals.

Dis-intermediated and localized markets are smaller in size and if they stay connected to each other are more robust in comparison to just one single large market. If one large market fails for whatever reason, it causes major disruptions. If a small market fails, it is still bad news for its participants, but the consequences stay local and limited. In our current economy, we tend to be willing to take the risk of few but large players in exchange for the efficiency gains that one or a few large markets provide, even if it comes with rare but disastrous consequences such as the financial crises in 2008. If a dis-intermediated economy is similarly efficient with very low transaction costs, the hope is that a trade-off between the robustness of markets and efficiency is no longer necessary. However, it is too early to judge if this is really the case. For example, it could well be the case that many connected local markets are prone to similar risks or that they come with other disadvantages.

Another potential advantage of localized markets is that they are more diverse. Ronald Coase, in "The Nature of the Firm" (1937), outlined the reason for the existence of firms: transactions costs within a firm are lower than on the market. This directly translates to the optimal size of a firm: as long as the transaction costs within the firm are lower than outside of the firm, it should grow – but when administrative costs within the firm become too large and render transactions within the firm more expensive than in the market, the firm should shrink. If blockchain technology leads to a reduction in transaction costs in the market, this directly translates into smaller companies. Lots of small shops each providing diverse goods and services with a unique flair compared to large chains that provide standardized goods and services immediately comes to mind. Currently, most people prefer the lower costs brought by standardization at the expense of individual and diverse options. But this could change in some degree, if smaller shops and businesses have access to similar levels of transaction costs and efficiency.

One market where such shifts are not conceivable is education. Education is much more than a market so changes to it can have powerful effects in our society. Currently, education is provided by teachers and professors who are embedded in institutions. While the teachers and professors directly engage with their students in day-to-day classroom life, and there is usually a large degree of freedom when it comes to the methods of teaching and setting priorities within the specifics of the curriculum, all major decisions on curricula, requirements to study time and achievements needed to receive a diploma, teaching schedules and hours, courses offered, and also the costs of studying are taken by the institutions and thus a given to teachers and students alike. This current system is a hybrid between reaping the benefits of centralized efficiency that are needed to provide comparable education and the freedom that is needed to foster talent and knowledge on an individual basis.

Blockchain technology could have disruptive effects on the current educational system. Large intermediaries, such as schools and universities provide homogeneous education at rather high costs that exclude many population groups in many countries. When education is provided directly by teachers and professors with institutions playing a much smaller role, education not only becomes more affordable and accessible but also verifiable. For example, it is possible to issue credentials on the blockchain instead of (or in addition to) paper-based certificates. This would drastically reduce the risk of manipulated certificates, empowering the students to have more control over their certificates by only granting reading rights to a potential employer during an application process but not afterwards. The potentially greater change might happen when students and educators are directly brought together through blockchain-based intermediaries and bypass traditional educational institutions. DLTs could help to establish players on the market for education that provide individualized educational offers at lower costs than traditional institutions. This could, for example, be fostered by corporations that use such educational players to define curricula that meet their specific requirements and give an employment guarantee for everyone passing all required exams.

The positives of such a shift in our educational system are straightforward. The most important potential is that education becomes more affordable leading to a higher inclusion rate and potentially higher social mobility. Education could also become more transparent and tailored to the specific needs of a student or capacities of a teacher. Donations or subsidies to help the education of a specific disadvantaged group would be much easier with less room for fraud and higher transparency. On the negative side, such a system faces the risk of being overtaken by large corporations in a way that misaligns their profit motives with the interest of society. It could also become so diverse that the qualifications are no longer comparable. Another risk is that it leads to either a two-tier education system or even the breakdown of state-run education, which would be the complete opposite of the original intention of dis-intermediating the education sector.

3.4 CENSORSHIP RESISTANCE AND PRIVACY

The need for privacy and censorship-resistant transactions have certainly played an important role in the development and the success of blockchains. The Universal Declaration of Human Rights states:

> Everyone has the right to freedom of opinion and expression; this right includes freedom to hold opinions without interference and to seek, receive and impart information and ideas through any media and regardless of frontiers
> (Article 19, Universal Declaration of Human Rights 1948)

While the advent of the internet held the promise for this aim by providing the architecture to make this vision reality, it did not fully succeed, as most websites and content are either hosted by or routed through intermediaries, who have the power to restrict and control content und thus free speech. Blockchain technology offers to give individuals the power of sending and receiving not only information but also value without surveillance or central control.

An important effect of such censorship resistance is that it fosters social mobility by preventing the exclusion of specific groups from vital services such as banking. Social mobility is not only a necessary condition for a fair and open society with more equal chances but also promises to enable disadvantaged communities to solve their own problems.

An important characteristic of public and open-source blockchain solutions is that they increase the costs of surveillance and thus provide a safeguard for the freedom of society. In their book *Blockchain Revolution*, Tapscott and Tapscott (2016) raise the concern that blockchain technology could be co-opted as a surveillance technology by governments and large corporations. Trying to stay in control, they argue, these large players will either build blockchain technology that they control or build surveillance technologies that allow them to surveil the information within existing blockchain systems. While it can be debated whether the motives are predominantly grounded in surveillance, it is convincing that large corporations are not focused on anonymity and users controlling their own data with their blockchain applications but are much more interested in gathering and monetarizing the data themselves.

Compare censorship resistance to the current situation in which WikiLeaks struggles with financial institutions to receive donations through the traditional payment system. WikiLeaks effectively was cut off from conventional financial services. The same is happening for other companies, industries and even countries that are deemed harmful by the established financial intermediaries. While it can be debated whether such embargoes are good or bad, the risk cannot be denied that the nature and targets of such embargoes could change with the political wind and potentially affect anybody. In a permissionless blockchain ecosystem, code ensures that certain individuals or groups are not preferred over others. Nodes do not give special privileges or impose conditions before verifying and executing transactions. This neutrality ensures that all are treated equally and are not abused by a centralized intermediary or gatekeeper. Yet, a decentralized network can be overtaken by centralized players as Google, Facebook and Amazon did with large parts of the internet. Blockchain technology, however, is not immune to a similar fate, because it is not unimaginable that users might prefer the convenience of centralized solutions over the censorship resistance of a P2P-based blockchain.

With blockchain-based intermediaries no one can be prevented from supporting a cause that is blacklisted by authorities, from supporting rebel groups that try to overthrow a regime, or support terrorist activities. While it raises law-enforcement issues or problems of implementing sanctions against unwanted behaviour, it also functions as a safety net for oppressed minorities and effectively anyone that could potentially fall victim to illegitimate repressions by a hostile regime. As a result, censorship-resistant technology shifts moral judgement from central authorities to the user of an application.

Governments have a vital interest in identity ledgers to track each member of the population from birth to death. Identity records are used to monitor movements, potential unlawful behaviour and especially income and wealth. This makes identity records a prerequisite to any fiscal and regulatory authority and also voting rights. Corporations also rely on the government-administered mass-population identity records, particularly banks and other financial firms, and thus play an integral role for surveillance of a population. It also means that not only governments but many large firms keep large repositories of identity records in centralized databases creating the risk of misuse of this data by either the company itself, which may lawfully or unlawfully sell the data to third parties, or by hackers that were attracted by the "honeypot" of data and can access the data if ineffective security measures are in place.

An extreme example of the misuse of centrally stored identity records is the Dutch population registry in the 1930s that contained information on addresses and religious beliefs. After Hitler's Nazi regime invaded the Netherlands and accessed the central registry, they were able to locate Jews living in the Netherlands and eventually deported and murdered most of them. To hypothesize further, at some point in the future it could become a crime to eat meat. In such a scenario anyone having purchased meat in the past could be prosecuted through evidence from detailed and personalized payment records that are kept by financial firms today. Distributed and encrypted data could ward off malicious intentions and powers – whether governments or large corporations.

On the other hand, technologies of private transactions and private information can be used as safe havens for criminals and hinder or prevent the prosecution of crime. Anonymous payments and wealth transfer will become easier with blockchains like Zcash, Monero or Dash allowing for crime, tax evasion and money laundering. At the same time, their privacy features support suppressed minorities and political opposition in repressive regimes. These privacy-oriented blockchain-based currencies are unlikely to overcome increasing surveillance by other digital technologies. But they provide a safe haven for tech-savvy activists. From the standpoint of the wider society it is an important ideological question as to whether such technologies should be used as safeguards against hostile takeovers and the misuse of the central data repositories, even if they do provide criminals with a tool. So far, society agrees, because cash is the oldest facilitator of anonymous transactions.

Overall, information, payment, and wealth privacy protects minority groups that are considered to be engaging in harmful behaviour by the majority; phrased this way it is clearly negative, but conversely it can be seen as a positive, if the majority opinion is prejudiced. Privacy cuts both ways.

Privacy is a necessary element for democracy. Consider the core element of every democratic (political) system: voting. Whenever the anonymity of voting is at risk, intimidation of voters and the manipulation of votes is possible. Blockchain technology promises to provide the means to increase voters' privacy and stop the potential for rigging or interfering with voting systems. It would enable voters to cast their votes from home and to potentially increase voting participation. In general, costs of staging an electoral ballot would be decreased.

Although blockchain-based identities offer great potential, they also come with risks. The process of transference between systems is a weak point: a break or non-connectivity between old and new systems of identity could create a mismatch between these systems. Blockchain-based systems could enable the use of multiple identities and thus potential fraud as well as complexities due to non-conformity with current rules, laws and procedures. Identities in distributed ledgers might also be more formable and less uniform than their traditional counterparts creating complexities and ambiguities. Depending on how serious and frequent such mismatches, complexities and ambiguities between the traditional and new identity records occur, the consequence could be a partial or even complete breakdown of trust in either system with potentially devastating consequences for the many activities in society. Any change in the way we treat our identity records has to be taken with precaution and with more than a safety net in place. In Chapter 4, we identify digital identities with a user-centric approach, so-called self-sovereign identities, as one of the major opportunities for blockchain technology, explain how they work and their advantages.

3.5 PROPERTY AND THE EMPOWERMENT OF THE INDIVIDUAL

Property rights and their protection are a fundamental element to modern society and play an integral part in the creation of today's wealth. Still, "property rights are not absolute and invariant, but rather denote social relationships that are subject continually to margins of contestation and potential change" (Wagner 2016: 164). As this quote indicates, property is not only freely transferable by the owner but can also be removed by force through theft, seizure or taxation. Every property owner has an interest in the credible recording of their ownership and its associated rights. These records are maintained in the form of centralized and usually paper-based ledgers. For example, in Germany every stock and financial security still needs to be backed by a paper-based document, although the trading and investing infrastructure overlay is all digital. No investor will ever see the share certificate of the stock that they own. Such paper-based foundations come with serious shortcomings as, for example, in the case of the share certificates: an ambiguity exists over who owns the share at a specific moment – most notably the moment before or after a dividend is paid. This created the multi-billion dollar "CumEx" tax loophole that has been exploited in Germany and other European countries for many years and has cost the taxpayers billions of euros. In general, such deficiencies of paper-based systems are numerous and it is widely accepted that its digital counterparts will boost efficiency.

Digital registries are large-scale solutions with a central institution as the gatekeeper and sole administrator that creates trust, legitimacy and the power of censorship and enforcement. DLT uses tokens to represent the assignment of rights to a defined asset (Antonopoulos 2017). Ownership can not only be validated through the blockchain, but its consensus algorithm can also depict any change of ownership almost instantaneously and does not involve a bank, governmental institution, or some other central intermediator. Smart contracts not only capture any change of ownership but also facilitate the exchange of property on the blockchain.

In countries where the documentation and thus protection of property rights is less well-organized, blockchain could enable the benefits of secure property transactions in the first place. Even if individuals in such countries have access to significant amounts of resources, when lacking proofs of ownership they cannot engage in economic transactions and invest their resources. This is where blockchain-based documentation of ownership has its highest potential.

To unfold its full potential, blockchain-based property also relies on trustworthy and accessible identity registers. But according to the World Bank, about 1.1 billion people do not have sufficient documents to prove their identity (Desai 2017). This is not only an issue for refugees seeking asylum and participation in Western countries, but also for providing a safe environment in the originating countries to invest resources and prevent corruption. It is here that blockchain-based identity solutions provide the highest value.

Similarly, health records of patients kept on the blockchain – instead of in, if at all, fragmented and centralized databases – could facilitate more accurate and quicker diagnoses and management of medicine. For example, in a case of an emergency in which it is physically impossible for someone to share their medical history personally, it is important that a doctor gets access, nonetheless. It is important to note that blockchain-based information should not always be either public or private but that there is a good argument for permissioned blockchains with multiple layers of reading and writing rights. It must be possible to keep parts of the data transparent to some nodes while keeping the rest hidden. This can be crucially important for applications in medicine but also other businesses and services that rely on confidentiality in transaction data but need to open it up for selected parties in specific situations as in the case of a medical emergency.

3.6 NEW MARKETS AND MARKETPLACES

There are heated discussions on the disruptive effect blockchain might have on various industries such as financial services (banks, insurance companies, payment providers, brokers), marketplaces and platform businesses (auction houses, social media, renting platforms), auditing and reporting (accounting, compliance, controlling) as well as on sovereign services (registers, notaries, voting). Such changes are certainly important; however, blockchain's impact might not simply be the disruption of existing industries but rather that it leads to the evolution of unknown products, services and markets that currently don't exist. Necessarily this involves a degree of speculation. However, we still want to engage in this discussion as we believe it is possible that new markets will shape our society even more than the disruption of existing markets.

History provides many situations in which new technologies not only disrupted existing industries but also led the advent of new products and markets that shaped our world. For example, the combustion engine disrupted the shipping industry, but it also led to the invention of automobiles, which shaped our world in a short period of time. The internet similarly disrupted the market for mail but also led to the emergence of social media. Blockchain may well also lead to the emergence of a completely new industry. The tokenization of physical and also virtual goods like patents, certificates, debt, credit, money, coupons, art or items in video games or virtual realities suggests many possibilities of new products and markets. As tokens can be easily exchanged, a new marketplace for all kinds of goods could be created. This comes with huge potential but also huge risks. When markets become more efficient, they prove positive stimulus to the economy, but there are also risks to market participants of negative societal externalities.

In the case of finance, the practices of largely unregulated financial markets in the 1920s certainly played a role in the Great Depression and economic downturn of the 1930s. The response to which was an increase in governmental oversight and regulation of financial markets. Today, financial markets are heavily regulated and manipulative practices play a much smaller role. However, these regulations only apply to the narrow definition of financial markets. They do not affect other markets such as the recently established market for cryptocurrencies or other new markets where blockchain-based tokens are exchanged. While such markets are largely regulated when it comes to dealing with fiat currencies and involve anti-money laundering (AML) and know-your-customer (KYC) checks, they are effectively still much less regulated than traditional financial markets that punish market manipulation and insider trading. When realizing losses, the victim can only sue in civil law – which requires proof of a causal effect between action and damage and a quantification of such damage. This is practically impossible and for this very reason specific laws preventing insider-trading, for example, are in place for financial markets. With newly established markets becoming increasingly similar to financial markets, it becomes important to repurpose some of these regulations for new marketplaces.

It is not inconceivable that some of these new markets might become so powerful as to shape and become integral parts of our society.

History has also demonstrated that jobs that can be automated are replaced by machines. In the past this has mainly affected lower-skilled, manual workers that were replaced by manufacturing or transportation machines. With self-executing smart contracts, comparably high-skilled workers could lose their jobs. These "digital machines" not only reduce transaction costs but can also replace intermediaries and then lead to job losses in these areas (Al-Saqaf & Seidler 2017). However, such higher-skilled workers might have less difficulty in adapting to the new situation and ac-quire the skills that allow them to find jobs in the newly developing areas.

Smart contracts also allow machine-to-machine interaction and contracts. Combined with a payment infrastructure this will facilitate completely new business models (Frey & Osborne 2016). For example, autonomous distributed markets could emerge that constantly allocate resources and organize production much more efficiently than currently. Autonomous machines like self-driving cars could independently act and automatically gather profits as well as cover their own maintenance and recycling costs. This echoes Marx's idea of more and more labour moving inside the machine with increasing levels of technology, with human la-bour playing an ever-decreasing role. At some point people might not be needed at all, neither to operate the machine nor to maintain, monitor nor even produce the machine in the first place. A major challenge, how-ever, will be – as with any new technology – to compensate those who will lose out or even be left behind by such a process.

An important aspect of any P2P and thus blockchain-based system is its lack of territorial borders. The usage of such systems will naturally lead to a globalized market in which, for example, workloads are distributed across the world. At the same time P2P networks and their reduced trans-action costs lead to decentralization that could empower local communi-ties and smaller businesses and potentially induce a shift in power balance within our society. Shifts in the power balance could occur within indus-tries, between companies and individuals (consumers), between individ-uals and governments, as well as between companies and governments.

Potential changes are not limited to first-world societies. In societies with less developed infrastructure, blockchains present lean systems for low-cost remittances from abroad, micropayments and access to financial services and investments for the unbanked. Blockchain's technical infrastructure facilitates local innovation, as start-ups and communities can develop and deploy applications, such as for local transportation. The potential impacts of increased financial inclusion could result in a fairer distribution of wealth and lay the foundation for flourishing local economies.

A *Forbes* article published in April 2018 was entitled "The future of social impact is ... Blockchain" and opened by asking the reader to imagine a technology that could improve the graduation rates of Nigerian girls, enable a musician to automatically convert part of their royalties into charity donations, coordinate the assignment of resources to refugees and thus create transparent aid organizations, and help homeowners to conserve electricity with a smart refrigerator. It would also make it easier to earmark funds for specific uses and thus allow more transparency in the usage of funds. This could raise the profile and effectiveness of charities working in developing countries. These are just a few examples of improving existing and establishing new markets and ways of interaction within society that either do not exist yet or have yet to reach their full potential, because trustworthy intermediaries cannot be found or are too expensive. In sum, all these applications and new markets could have a huge socio-economic impact.

3.7 CRYPTO-SECESSION: THE MOST DISRUPTIVE POTENTIAL OF DISTRIBUTED LEDGER TECHNOLOGY

Fostered by technological progress, institutions and societies evolve and change over time to adapt to changing conditions. From an evolutionary perspective, different institutional structures within societies and societies themselves compete for adherents and power. Societies and institutions thus act under a selection pressure that originates from individuals having the choice to either act within one or the other institutional system. Each system allows, at least to some degree, for changes induced from within and thus for those acting under its regime to voice concerns. From an evolutionary point of view, the greater pressure, however, comes from individuals choosing to exit either because of displeasure or because a different system promises a better environment. Within an institutional system, there is the tendency to improve its conditions in order to compete with other systems as well as to reduce the competitive pressure by limiting the choices to exit either by imposing costs of change (think, for example, an exit taxation when leaving a country) or by force (e.g. capital controls).

In a physical world where people cannot easily leave the places they live in, any political or institutional system must aim to include everyone in the region where it prevails. In a non-physical world (or in a physical world where exits and entries are not prohibitively expensive), a different approach could have competing systems that evolve side-by-side and are permeable. As Buchanan and Faith pointed out back in 1987, the territorial aspect is no longer compulsory in today's society. This puts more pressure on the systems to evolve in the interest of its members so as to prevent them from "voting with their feet". Blockchain-based permissionless systems with censorship resistance, like Bitcoin, can serve as the fundamental layer that allows the creation of such a situation of dynamic self-evolving and competing systems, especially in the digital world, by reducing switching costs and thus effectively enabling exits and entries between systems. Individuals who are not served by the old system or potentially even oppressed become empowered by new censorship-resistant systems. This empowerment of individuals eases exits from one system and entries into another system and thus shifts the power balance between institutions and individuals as well as between competing institutions. For example, when record-keeping is conducted on permissionless ledgers instead of centralized and monopolized repositories, then an institution cannot use their monopoly on record-keeping to punish those who want to leave the system.

The potential of blockchains enabling the movement out of existing institutional systems is coined "crypto-secession" (Allen *et al.* 2018) with individuals not changing their geographical region but simply retreating to a virtual world. Blockchains enable such a process by providing virtual ways for economic, social and even political engagement through the use of censorship-resistant transactions and smart contracts that allow the creation of decentralized and potentially autonomous organizations. Such a new space competes with existing institutional arrangements and, if they find more effective ways of solving economic and non-economic problems, individuals will consider to crypto-secede from existing institutions. Figure 3.9 shows such a process. The left square depicts the traditional world where everyone is part of the same institutional system. The right square shows the same society where some members (crypto-) secede into a new (blockchain-based) system that functions outside the traditional system. Two of these members rely exclusively on this new system, whereas one member is part of both the new and the old system and thus acts as a connection between the systems. By adding the new (blockchain-based) system, the society becomes institutionally more varied and complex. This could make it more productive and resilient but also prone to internal conflicts.

Traditional ledger systems are not trustless but are centred around an institution that has made large and often irreversible investments into building trust (Davidson *et al.* 2018). It is the recording of data in siloed, permissioned ledgers that gives power to these institutions and allows them to accumulate rents to finance the initial investment. Institutions can use their control over data to function as gatekeepers that can grant or decline access and establish rules (including payments) for it. For example, an entrepreneur who starts a company is not allowed to operate until they register the company in a central ledger and has additional licences required for their specific business. This raises the threat of abuse of this power and trust that the license-granting institution has built. As long as the majority is served, there is the potential to

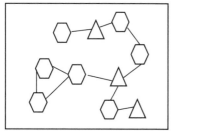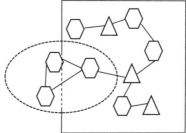

Figure 3.9 The development of a blockchain-based system in addition to a traditional institutional system allows parts of a society to "crypto-secede"

Source: adapted from Allen *et al.* (2018).

discriminate minorities. These minorities are the exact societal actors who could secede.

An important part of governmental institutions is to maintain stable identity ledgers and records. These are as uniform as possible to ease their usage, but also to facilitate the collection of taxes and fees as well as the targeting of specific regulatory policies. This uniformity of, for example, ID documents makes identity theft a concerning issue, especially when it is mandatory to submit ID documents to access more and more services for regulatory compliance reasons (such as AML). While blockchain could not remove the need to verify an identity it can, at least, remove the need to store such identities in centralized databases. With blockchain-based identities citizens could manage their identity and give only temporary access to it, when verification is necessary. This would also empower individuals and ease a potential crypto-secession. Blockchain technology thus makes it more feasible for individuals to exit political-socio-economic systems and elect to join other, emerging systems that allow to keep and verify not only identities but all sorts of public records without a centralized authority.

At the same time, blockchain can also empower existing institutions. First, to interact in modern societies, individuals demand secure and stable property rights including the right to use and exchange property and provide security from theft, corruption and manipulation and be able to punish or exclude those that undermine or violate property rights. Second, interaction in society further requires the use of communication. Third, interaction requires record keeping of property to prove their existence and allocation. An institutional system must provide access to technologies that allow such interaction. The easier and more cost-efficient these are, the more interaction between members of a society is fostered and the more attractive the system is. Blockchain is a technology that provides security in transaction and integrity of records in a cost-efficient way. With advancements towards scalability and usability, it is to be expected that record-keeping on blockchains and the range of interactions that can be conducted with blockchain-based systems will increase. This potentially increases the competitive advantage of institutional systems embracing blockchain technology.

4

Applications of blockchain technology in different domains

As indicated in the previous chapters, there are broad application potentials for blockchain technology. It is a comparably young technology, which is developing and constantly progressing, and which could be deployed in almost every sector. It is quite possible that some of the most exciting and innovative applications of the technology have not yet been considered. Smart contracts in combination with micro-transactions will enable futuristic smart applications. For example, hotel rooms or parking spaces that are autonomously billed and paid for in real time, or media articles that are billed per single-word read. However, one must always be aware that while the blockchain itself is a theoretically error-free system, such applications always require data transmissions from external sources (known as oracles). There is a danger that information could be manipulated here. Depending on the case, the blockchain solution is only as good as the level of trust in the oracle that provides data. In turn, this creates new business potential for insurance companies to insure such risks.

In the hunt for new ideas and applications, there are some simple questions that should always be asked initially: is there an existing intermediary that could be eliminated by using blockchain or cryptocurrency? Are certain applications required to document or collateralize processes because participants in a market or transaction are reluctant to do so?

Currency and remittances are obvious applications that fulfil these criteria. It is no surprise that the inventor of the blockchain introduced a cryptocurrency as the first application, when the effects of the Great Financial Crisis were taking hold. A classic bank account is just centrally deposited with a bank and when money is transferred, various intermediaries (the initiator's bank and the target bank) are always involved. With cryptocurrency the degree of private autonomy increases, but this also leads to an increased risk. Banks have deposit protection and users are insured against theft. This is not the case with cryptocurrency. So there is a trade-off between independence and security, which comes with fees and external monitoring. For cross-border transfers, the use of blockchain-based value transfers is immediately clear. While classic service providers in this area charge extremely high fees, blockchain transactions can be sent quickly and securely across national borders. However, exchanging values from the blockchain into the respective national currency is problematic. Using Bitcoin as an example, users are dependent on their ability to exchange these into their local currency (or on the vendor of a good or service to accept Bitcoin directly).

Clearly there are still many problems that need to be solved, but the respective potential is evident. On the one hand, the technology promises a more efficient or less expensive system in the future and, on the other hand, conventional providers identify this progressive change as a danger to their business model. There are companies that generally refuse and prohibit use of blockchain and others that have adapted or extended their business models to it. A lack of development and improvement by existing established entities leads to more innovative approaches by new emerging firms that approach and eventually take over these stagnant processes.

While it is still unclear how blockchain technology will develop in the future, we will present selected applications that either clearly offer potential efficiency gains, open up completely new markets or describe potential advantages and disadvantages of the blockchain. This chapter is intended to give the reader further understanding of applications and an inspiration for what might be possible. Blockchain can bring about a digital revolution in the digital world. The following examples provide a suitable basis to grasp the potential reach of blockchain-based applications:

1. Central bank digital currency (CBDC) has the potential to transform money into a public good, resulting in significant potential economic growth due to lower transaction costs. Such solutions are being actively worked on by governments and future implementations are realistic.
2. Energy markets and infrastructure that comprise system-critical, highly regulated markets that can only be disrupted slowly.
3. Self-sovereign identity in which people control their digital identity and data. This could lead to a structural shift of digital interaction.
4. Capital markets for new business models such as the tokenization of digital values – decentralized finance (DeFi). Conventional clearing and settlement processes could be dis-intermediated
5. Gambling can be decentralized eliminating the need for casino operators (and associated fees), making it more transparent, with positive effects on regulation and law enforcement.

4.1 CENTRAL BANK DIGITAL CURRENCY (CBDC)

A digital currency offered by a central bank possesses considerable potential. As a state payment infrastructure, prevailing transaction costs could be completely eliminated. Payment service providers that currently operate, some of which levy high fees, would no longer be required and the costs saved could potentially lead to a reduction in the prices of goods and services. There are conceivable advantages for society as a whole, but CBDC would have to be introduced gradually against the backdrop of established structures in the financial sector. In this section we explain the concept of CBDC and why blockchain is a suitable, basic technology for its application.

The term CBDC is not well-defined; its concepts most often consist of a digital form of money issued by a central bank, which can be used as a store of value or as a medium of exchange (Coeuré & Loh 2018). According to the Bank of Canada, CBDC describes electronically stored monetary value, which represents the liability of a central bank or can be used for payments (Engert & Fung 2017). The Bank of England refers to CBDC as "a central bank granting universal, electronic, 24/7, national-currency-denominated and interest-bearing access to its balance sheet" (Barrdear & Kumhof 2016: 8). Numerous states are actively exploring CBDC (White *et al.* 2017), including Sweden (Häring 2017), Estonia (Meyer 2017), Japan (Reilly 2017), the United Arab Emirates (Carvalho 2017), Canada (Wilkins 2016), Russia (Seddon & Arnold 2018) and China (Chao & Chen 2017) among others.

The use of blockchain technology is not strictly required for the operation of a CBDC system. However, the implementation of blockchain as the backbone for CBDC would have potential advantages, especially practical ones that ensure the resilience of the system. The maintenance of a blockchain for the purpose of a CBDC could be conducted solely by the central bank in question, which sustains all copies of the blockchain itself, public institutions acting as independent nodes in a permissioned network or in combination with the involvement of private-sector third-party service providers (Barrdear & Kumhof 2016). The degree of transparency allows a central bank to monitor any cash flow at any time, which generates additional benefits from a regulator's point of view. Unlike cash, the level of anonymity is low. However, this is directly related to the design of the blockchain infrastructure.

A central bank's role is that of an authoritative financial supervisor and controller. They conduct monetary and macroprudential policy independently, regulate banks, financial services and provide financial resources themselves as lenders of last resort to their national banking system. These instruments allow central banks to stabilize national (or multinational) currencies, indirectly affect unemployment rates and steer inflation. Central banks typically issue liabilities, one of which is physical bank notes, the other is electronic central bank deposits, often referred to as reserves or settlement balances (Engert & Fung 2017). While bank notes are a bearer instrument intended for anonymous widespread use, access to central bank reserves is limited to qualified financial institutions. A digital currency provided by a central bank for the use by the general public would represent a complementary digital form of physical cash. As such digital currency would likely be accounted for in the respective central banks' ledgers, the provision of digital currency would implicitly constitute an extension of the availability of central bank reserves. Rather than maintaining a centralized central bank ledger, digital currency could alternatively be issued in a decentralized manner (Engert & Fung 2017).

Figure 4.1 visualizes the taxonomy of money (Bech & Garratt 2017) and the respective categorization of CBDC. Different forms of money are displayed by their combination of the four key properties: issuer (central bank or other); form (digital or physical); accessibility (restricted or widely); and technology (token- or account-based) (Coeuré & Loh 2018). The latter property distinguishes cash and cryptocurrencies as token-based in contrast to most forms of commercial bank money that is account-based (Mersch 2017). The taxonomy presents three different forms of CBDC: CB general purpose tokens, CB wholesale tokens and CB general purpose accounts: Coeuré and Loh (2018) differentiate

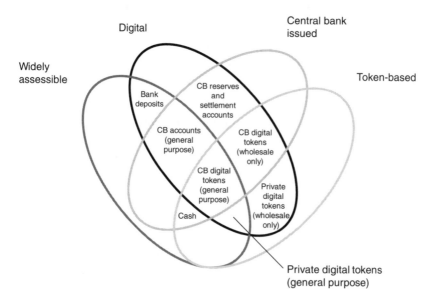

Figure 4.1 Visualization of the scopes of CBDC

Source: adapted from Bech & Garrat (2017).

payments into retail and wholesale. While the general-purpose token envisages wide accessibility, the wholesale token is used for high-value and high-priority transactions in the wholesale segment. However, such a distinction might not be necessary with CBDC's introduction, because an adequate blockchain design for CBDC would most probably be capable of processing certain numbers of transactions, which makes it unnecessary to prioritize transactions according to their value. CB general purpose accounts imply the provision of every citizen with an account at the central bank, similar to those of commercial banks. In contrast to the other design models, this would not imply the creation of tokens to be used for payments, but either central bank accounts serve as a store of value only, or payments using central bank accounts simply result in balance-sheet shifts across digital accounts.

The motivations for central banks issuing CBDC can be to account for changing technological developments, reducing the costs of money (i.e. cash) management, inducing more effective monetary policy and to establish more efficient settlement processes. Issuing a general-purpose digital currency would create another instrument for central banks, if its introduction is accompanied with a decline in the use of cash. The widespread adoption and use of general-purpose tokens would allow central banks to pass the policy rate onto money and lending markets more effectively. In stressful economic times, when an economy is close to recession, extending the quantitative amount of money in circulation motivates citizens to spend and thereby strengthen the economy. The concept of helicopter money (Friedman 1969), which distributes newly created central bank money to the private sector and citizens, is a feasible monetary instrument if citizens have an account with the central bank and general-purpose digital tokens are used as means of payment. However, the degree of transparency may also lead to other states or citizens being able to observe all payments and monetary measures. Accordingly, appropriate read and write permissions should be defined so that only intended entities can view information.

Another motivation for central banks to issue CBDC would be to decrease the cost of money management. Issuing physical bank notes involves the costs of designing, producing, distributing and destroying money. Creating a digital form of verifiable money would reduce the costs of cash handling (Fung & Halaburda 2016). Moreover, CBDC is potentially superior to existing retail and wholesale payment systems in terms of efficiency and safety. For retail payments, this includes P2P and point of sale transactions. For the wholesale segment and interbank payments, faster settlement and extended settlement hours would be feasible (Barrdear & Kumhof 2016). In the retail sector, consumers would profit from a payment system that is more efficient and less costly than existing private-sector solutions, such as PayPal, as the exclusion of payment service providers would cut fees for merchants. These costs are commonly passed onto consumers through higher product prices, whereas lower transaction fees could result in lower product prices.

By issuing a CBDC, central banks can account for recent advances in technology and preserve the effectiveness of monetary policy and thus their role of ensuring financial stability. If cryptocurrencies on public blockchain networks or private-sector initiatives, such as Facebook's Libra project, experience wide adoption, central-bank influence and the effectiveness of its financial interventions may decrease. Public blockchain systems are not owned by any accountable entity and if they increase in adoption and replace existing payment systems, central banks have no control over these payment systems and thus cannot fulfil their task of overseeing them. A failure of public blockchain systems or privately issued cryptocurrencies for payments could potentially result in a loss of trust in the technology and even adverse economic effects (Fung & Halaburda 2016). In this respect, there is a clear incentive on the part of regulatory bodies either to prevent such systems or to set them up themselves.

Along with an introduction of CBDC, increased competition within the private sector would likely occur, as a CBDC represents liabilities with the central bank that are potentially more trusted by consumers than liabilities with commercial banks which can go bankrupt in times of financial crisis. This is especially the case if the CBDC is interest-bearing. In this case, consumers would earn interest for holding

CBDC with a central bank account. The interest rate could reflect the policy rate, which the central bank applies to commercial banks to lend money. Thus, the business models of commercial banks, as well as the overall role of central banks would change eventually. An increased substitution of financial asset investments towards interest-bearing CBDC would be feasible. One possible solution to this problem could be to limit the amount of personal money in digital currency at a central bank. Private individuals, for example, could be limited to holding up to 10,000 (digital) euros or dollars in the central bank account and would have to use regular banks for amounts above this. Similar offers could be designed for companies, with greater complexity based on different sizes and cash flows.

Developing a CBDC system would require a sound analysis of the extent to which anonymity of usage and transparency of the blockchain is provided to the general public. Anonymity would conflict with the concept of an interest-bearing CBDC. It would need to be evaluated when evidence is strong enough for institutions to reveal the identities behind certain accounts. As the transparency of the blockchain would allow users to observe the amount of money deposited with the central bank or on an individual wallet software, this feature would most probably not be advantageous. It can be assumed that consumers would rather not expose their account balances with those they interact with. But, on the other hand, a certain level of transparency must be provided in order for the public to observe that adequate and truthful processing is going on inside the system. The programmability of blockchains offers a direct solution here. It would be conceivable that anonymity of payments up to a certain amount and/or volume of payments would be guaranteed and only then would a central bank have access to them. This would guarantee autonomy and privacy and at the same time allow the bank access to suspicious cases. In addition, such anonymity could be lifted under certain conditions, in order to comply with court proceedings or the urgent investigation of potential criminal activity, for example.

Employing a blockchain to underpin a CBDC would deliver certain advantages in contrast to pure account-based CBDC. These include a token-based solution that can circulate freely among private individuals and companies, other than being a simple balance-sheet transaction with central bank accounts. While the latter concept would bear no transaction costs, a freely floating token would be more akin to cash and reduce the actual costs of money management. If the CBDC is widely accepted it could replace cash. Furthermore, a distributed system of validators, be they incentivized "miners", commissioned private-sector players or state institutions, creates a resilient system and reduces the threats of a single-point-of-failure. Each transaction is auditable in a potentially anonymous way, while anonymity could be revoked if any criminal activity is indicated. The application of blockchain technology for CBDC has further been found to potentially improve the prosecution and prevention of criminal activities such as tax fraud, money-laundering and identity theft (Steinmetz 2017).

A blockchain design for underpinning CBDC would most probably be permissioned, so as to have trusted validators of transactions and blocks. Accordingly, resource-intensive consensus mechanisms could be simplified to the benefit of the scalability of transaction throughput, while maintaining a transparent and verifiable processing of the validators. With a certain level of transparency of the validation processes, every faulty or suspicious transaction and pattern could be traced back to its origin as well as the entities that proposed or falsely validated them. Thus, a state-initiated CBDC could potentially imply increased confidentiality that improves the trust towards institutions in general, because of the high-level transparency it affords.

State institutions can create CBDC as open-source technology and provide an infrastructure to the public and private sector. Concepts of providing freely accessible data for the private and public sector relate to government-as-a-platform (O'Reilly 2011), which could potentially be extended by a CBDC-blockchain infrastructure (Nicholson 2017) that facilitates compliant and efficient transaction settlements. Accordingly, a state-initiated and maintained blockchain infrastructure could potentially be extended to facilitate smart contracts as well. Such a concept would enable private-sector players to innovate on the provided infrastructure and create and deploy additional applications and services.

Such enhanced functionality of a state-run blockchain could also improve the security, efficiency and costs of other processes relevant for public services, for example, land registration, voting, identity management, supply-chain traceability, health-care records, proxy voting, corporate registrations, taxation, and entitlements management (White *et al.* 2017), some of which are addressed in the following sections.

CBDC systems would most probably differ from public blockchain systems. Rather than being trust-free by decentralizing control, CBDC designs are focused on concentrating and maintaining control by central banks. While the application of blockchain technologies in this realm is potentially advantageous in terms of efficiency, it could also complement and underpin state-surveillance systems which is contrary to blockchain's originally intended use. Following this, a sound analysis of how these systems can preserve the rights of individual users to be protected from manipulation and arbitrariness is necessary as the solution to this will influence public acceptance and usage of these types of complementary currencies.

In conclusion, concepts of CBDCs still face some challenges, but their introductions are foreseeable, as the economic and social potentials are enormous. Central banks are actively researching the issue and similar private-sector efforts, such as Facebook's project Libra, will accelerate further research and future implementation.

4.2 ENERGY MARKETS AND INFRASTRUCTURE

Blockchain technology could be used to increase the overall efficiency of energy markets and thereby help to reduce waste and pollution. The main potential lies in decentralizing the markets, enabling P2P trading, secure data transmission and in incentivizing market participants to flatten peaks of energy demand and supply. A blockchain-based smart grid in combination would be the key to this ambitious endeavour.

In an interference-free energy network, providers must react flexibly to the temporal fluctuations of demand and be able to compensate for differences in demand. The required balancing power is traded at very high prices, especially to cover short-term fluctuations. Inefficiencies that result from this process could be drastically reduced by involving all consumers in the short-term balancing of energy load and supply. By using blockchain, an integrated and standardized energy market could be created. Its underlying price mechanism would offer all consumers the incentive to participate in the process of market compensation. Therefore, the peaks of energy load could be reduced and gaps in the allocation of energy avoided. As a result, the balancing power could be reduced without interfering with the security of supply. Ultimately this would lead to cost savings and an improvement in the environmental balance.

An integrated and standardized energy market offers enormous potential for efficiency gains compared to the current state of the market. With the help of a variable price that depends on the current demand and supply of energy, incentives to consume energy could effectively be shifted towards times, for example, night time, and make its consumption more cost-effective. Additionally, variable prices offer incentives for implementing intelligent energy storage systems. In such systems, energy is called on at the most favourable moment, stored and fed back into the system when the energy demand and therefore the price is at its peak. Through the connection to the blockchain, the potential for load displacement and energy storage could be managed in a decentralized way. This enables owners of the corresponding facilities to make these externally accessible and manageable. In addition to the traditional electricity purchase agreement, a supplier could offer their customers the possibility of connecting private energy storage via blockchain.

Smart meters are intelligent electricity and gas meters that act as an interface between consumers and the energy grid. A smart meter determines the energy consumption within a certain time interval and transmits the collected data immediately. Household smart meters communicate internally with all energy-consuming devices and machines of an energy consumer and externally with all energy providers. The consumption of a household is recorded by the smart meter and automatically forwarded to the energy supplier. The latter can then use this data, in compliance with the legal framework. Producers of energy share the current and future energy supply with other energy providers and with consumers. A problem here is the transmission speed. For example, smart meters (in Germany) transmit data at 15-minute intervals. This length of time interval precludes standardization in the short term, since other methods of remote monitoring and control are carried out within seconds.

A smart grid is an intelligent energy network that integrates the consumption and feed-in of all connected market participants into an efficient and sustainable system to ensure lower energy losses and higher availability. A prerequisite for the successful introduction of a smart grid is that information about the power grid is always up to date. Up-to-date information available in a timely manner is essential to managing loads sensibly or to evaluate the capacity utilization of individual segments. The underlying sensor technology (like blockchain) and the corresponding IT infrastructure thus form the basis for intelligent power grids.

By using blockchain technology and smart meters, an owner of an electric car can connect the car battery to the blockchain, whereupon the car could automatically buy and sell (or store and deliver) energy when it is not in use. The amount of battery capacity used for this purpose can be determined by a blockchain-based smart contract or via a centralized solution that transmits the information to the blockchain-based market. Users can make full use of the battery if they do not need the car or use it in a limited way, to make sure the car battery is always charged (e.g. at least 50 per cent). Theoretically, this concept can be applied to any electrical storage device and to any device whose use is variable in time. In addition to the offer for private customers, such a concept also represents a business model for business customers – possibly this model is currently most feasible for (large) businesses or corporate customers.

Another potential application of the blockchain is the transfer and storage of data. Data itself, authorizations and access protocols can be stored, assigned and automated via blockchain.

An energy market linked via a blockchain and smart meters allows the energy load to be shifted and energy to be stored efficiently, thus enabling a reduction in energy consumption costs, an increase in supplier profits and an improvement in the environmental balance. At the same time, there are different hurdles along the way, some of which include:

- Existing business models could be superseded that form an opposition to change.
- Existing equipment, especially in households, is not designed to react to time-dependent electricity costs; an exchange of these devices is usually not worthwhile in the short term.
- Consumers are sceptical about publishing their consumption data.
- The monitoring and control of power generation and supply is still too inflexible.

Therefore, it would be unrealistic to integrate the entire energy market in the short term. However, its gradual introduction could be key, as this would overcome these hurdles incrementally. In the long term, an integrated energy market has to become the future of power generation.

In the short term, established processes of energy trading could be supported by blockchain rather than being fully replaced. Silo formation and individual data exchange could be settled via a blockchain that acts as a secure support mechanism for the entire market. However, the standardization of mechanisms and processes is a highly relevant factor for the energy market that itself is regulated to a very high degree, and blockchain still lacks the level of standardization required.

A blockchain for the energy sector requires very specific characteristics and qualities that the technology, especially public blockchains, may not be able to ensure today, as pointed out by Merz (2016). Table 4.1 shows an overview of the major characteristics and qualities lacking in public blockchains.

Public blockchain infrastructures, like Bitcoin or Ethereum, are equipped with units that can be used to process monetary transactions. Therefore, theoretically the process of directly implementing payments into a blockchain-based energy network does not represent an obstacle. Although Bitcoin and Ether are volatile, stable coins (i.e. tokens that resemble fiat currencies like the US dollar or euro) are suitable options for a regulated market, in which participants do not want to be exposed to price volatility risks. A blockchain-based energy market for data exchange could also be developed so that the settlement of payments is automatically attached to transactions. Invoices could be automatically

Table 4.1 Characteristics and requirements for public blockchain systems for their use in energy markets

Characteristic	Requirement
Availability	Nodes should be able to reconnect to the network within a few minutes or a complementary node should be put online as soon as a different node fails.
Immutability	Specific long-term commitments that do not change over the course of time should be immutably broadcasted to the blockchain. For different processes, data becomes obsolete after a specific time period, which results in the irrelevant storage of data across nodes. The partial deletion or cut-off of transactions could be a way to boost efficiency of the system.
Scalability	The blockchain should be able to process up to 100 transactions per second in times of high traffic.
Block time	The current market structure is slow, which is why block settlement after 30–60 seconds could be sufficient. Yet, for a (futuristic) truly efficient market, block times would have to be much faster.
Trustless	Irrelevant, as node operators are trusted. In the highly regulated energy market, all users need to be known.
Data volume	The monthly volume of data should be multiple terabytes.
Smart contracts	Not a necessity, as 1) the exchange and synchronizing of data is of greatest relevance and 2) network participants are known. Still only a possibility.
Consensus	Methods like proof-of-stake (PoS), Byzantine fault tolerance (BFT), state channels (i.e. second-layer transaction-processing) or reputation-based methods are favourable, as proof-of-work (PoW) may be too ineffective.
Accessibility and (pseudo)-anonymity	Data of market participants cannot be accessible to everyone but only to authorized users, like entities that are directly involved in a trade with each other or the regulatory authority. Data protection has a high relevance, as market participants compete in the system
Payments	Not a necessity, but an option.
Currency	Not a necessity but an option.

Source: adapted from Merz (2016).

issued via the blockchain and payments could be automatically triggered at specific pre-defined times. Blockchain-based payments in an energy market would require market participants to use digital currency. Established institutions, like banks, or specific fintech start-ups could act as market intermediaries that handle such processes as a service.

In terms of energy trading, current systems require brokers and centralized trading venues, where supply and demand of energy is settled. As blockchain technology enables secure transactions between individuals that do not have to trust each other, intermediaries and centralized trading could be disrupted. Projects like 0x (0x.org) develop protocols for the decentralized trading of blockchain assets. By Q2 2019, over 13 different decentralized exchanges are using the 0x protocol to enable P2P exchange of crypto assets on the internet. Traders can directly connect to the blockchain and exchange assets with other users. The Enerchain project (enerchain.ponton.de) went live in May 2019 and offers a decentralized marketplace for *inter alia* energy trading. Prosumers, consumers and suppliers are able to directly trade energy with each other without a centralized entity. Andoni *et al.* (2019) provide an overview for the potential impact of blockchain technology on energy company operations (see Table 4.2).

Traditional processes will inevitably be disrupted by the implementation of blockchain as a basic technology to provide an underlying security and settlement layer for data and/or payments. Figure 4.2 provides a visualization of one possible step towards integrating blockchain technology into the energy market. Traditional processes involve manual processing and a high level of communication to ensure the validity of information in the network. Information is stored at an individual level and third-parties, like brokers, trading agents and bankers are required to enable a functioning market. A blockchain-based market will not (in the near future) eliminate all intermediaries but provide a common shared database that enables anonymity by design. For example, every regular user can monitor that transactions are happening but can only fully identify the underlying information of their own transactions. The traditional energy company could become obsolete, as all information would be directly shared across the blockchain and there would be no need for an

Table 4.2 Characteristics and potential impacts of blockchain technology in the energy market

Characteristic	Potential Impact
Billing	Invoices can be automatically sent to consumers and other market participants. This could enable additional options, such as pay-as-you-go solutions or prepaid energy for consumers.
Sales and marketing	Profiles and preferences of energy consumers and producers can be captured (and analyzed) at a higher detail level.
Trading and markets	Blockchain-based trading of energy can improve conditions for wholesale market management, commodity trading and risk management. Additionally, green-energy certificates can be made tradeable, providing incentives for clean energy.
Automation	The self-production and self-consumption of energy can be improved via the implementation of local energy markets and the technology can improve control and governance over decentralized (micro-)grids and markets.
Smart-grid applications and data transfer	The blockchain can be used for data transfer, storage and transmission and ensure (pseudo-)anonymity of market participants.
Grid management	The network management and asset management can be supported by a blockchain architecture.
Security and identity management	Cryptographic methods, like anonymization of transactions, enable both security and identity of users and data.
Sharing of resources	The distributed network structure of blockchains can provide a fitting solution for efficient sharing solutions, like EV-charging infrastructure or data-sharing.
Competition	Via the use of smart contracts, processes can be simplified, made faster and more efficient.
Transparency	All transactions are immutably stored on the blockchain and can be made available to regulators or auditors.

Source: adapted from Adoni *et al.* (2019).

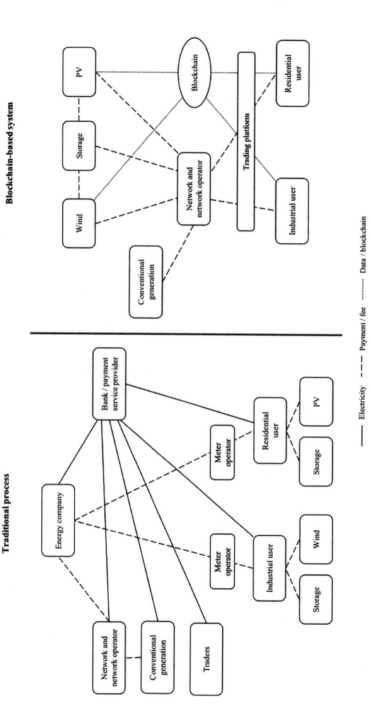

Figure 4.2 Traditional and blockchain-based processes in an energy market

Source: adapted from PwC (2016).

intermediary that processes information. This is only a futuristic theoretical assumption, as (1) energy markets are highly regulated and (2) there is no single energy market. Due to timing and transportation, various different energy markets exist that are split based on geolocation, time of settlement and quantity of units. These markets are connected with each other and it is somewhat unrealistic that a blockchain-based system could take over all relevant processes of energy companies regarding the interconnectivity between these markets.

An integratively networked and standardized energy market offers enormous efficiency potential compared to today's state. A variable price depending on energy demand and energy supply offers incentives to shift one's own energy requirements over time. Another example is energy storage: variable prices offer incentives for the construction of intelligent energy storage systems. Such storage demands energy at the cheapest moment, stores it and releases it when the energy demand and thus the price are greatest. The connection to the blockchain enables potentials for load shifting and energy storage to be mapped in a decentralized network. This enables owners of corresponding systems to make these externally accessible and manage them. For example, an electricity supplier could offer its customers the connection to private energy storage facilities via the blockchain in addition to the traditional contract for the purchase of electricity.

Energy markets are subject to extremely tight regulation because of the system's importance. The implementation of new, innovative approaches in this market therefore faces various administrative and legal challenges that will inevitably delay processes. In contrast to other sectors, the greatest benefit may not come from the blockchain alone but from the intelligent linking of various technologies.

In principle, blockchain technology is suitable for the secure storage and transmission of data and for P2P trading. To operate an extensive energy network and an energy market de-centrally on a blockchain and to create a smart grid in combination with other technologies is a vision that requires further research, but its implementation is still a long way off in reality.

4.3 SELF-SOVEREIGN IDENTITY

Digital identities, i.e. their security and accessibility, are a complex topic. In today's world of centralized systems, data must be repeatedly entered (i.e. login credentials) for ensuring security. Google, Facebook or Paypal have enabled login facilities – where users can use their data stored centrally on these platforms to access other pages. Individuals are faced with a trade-off between data sovereignty that is imbued with complexity or the loss of control over their own data through simplification of processes. Blockchain offers the chance to circumvent this trade-off. The decentralized anchoring of personal data, which can be partially released, opens up the opportunity for a simple and secure use of digital identities.

The meaning of identity and what it consists of has been reshaped in recent decades, as more aspects of everyday life are affected by, organized through or have completely shifted onto the internet and its platforms. Accordingly, a digital identity is shaped and complemented by numerous pieces of digital data, which have been submitted online by individuals. A "digital identity corresponds to the electronic information associated with an individual in a particular identity system" (Bhargav-Spantzel *et al.* 2006). Such systems are employed by service providers for authenticating and authorizing users to access their services. Moreover, an identity today comprises data, which has not been submitted by an individual directly, but rather has been assembled from analyzed data pieces. Such secondary identity information can be compiled from psychographics – information extracted from individual usage, interests and purchase behaviour, to create custom and personal profiles: "Identity is not only what you want to reveal about yourself, but also what others conclude, believe, and find out about yourself" (Alpár *et al.* 2011: 5). Such digital data adds to the traditional sense of identity that is authenticated through government-issued identity documents, driver licences, insurance cards and passports.

Identity management is the sum of all processes and involves technologies for creating, managing and using digital identities. These processes encompass the setup of a user identity, managing its access to the specific service and the maintenance of identity profiles. The principles of identity solutions must be secure and resilient, interoperable, privacy-enhancing and voluntary to the public, as well as cost-effective and easy to use. However, the historic evolution of identity-management systems has not produced a generally accepted standard or concept. Rather, identity and its management in the internet as of today is complex, inconvenient, not privacy-centric and insecure (Alpár *et al.* 2011).

What comes with this deficient practice in identity management is the serious risk of identity theft (Bhargav-Spantzel *et al.* 2006). Since the widespread adoption of the internet, an increasing number of sensible processes are conducted online and sensible information is digitized, which increases individuals' exposure to the risk of identity theft. As described earlier in Chapter 2 on client–server architecture, individuals are often not themselves personally responsible for the exposure and misuse of their data. Data breaches and leaks have become a characteristic of our time: centrally stored data silos containing sensitive (and valuable) personal data are a single point of failure and therefore an interesting target for attacks. A blockchain is resistant to such data breaches and leaks, as it has no central point of failure.

The organizations that collect such data are arguably offering services which are valuable for users. This, and a lack of knowledge of the underlying value of the data transmitted, is why users voluntarily submit their data (and, in some cases, there is a lack of alternatives). However, there is an inherent conflict in the present structure of interaction between users and commercial service providers: individuals are at most seen as potential customers. That is, the providers and collectors of data use it to optimize and personalize their offerings, sell and share data for profits or predict future trends (Schwab *et al.* 2011). Compromised data silos exemplify the dilemma with identity management from both the perspective of the user as well as of the data collectors. Users have no control over their data, whereas companies create single points of failure by collecting and centrally storing such data. Incidents such as breaches at Capital One or Equifax have led to social security numbers of a broad swathe of the US population being illegally available for purchase on the internet.

The idea of a digital identity has been evolving for decades. Allen outlines its development phases from centralized identities to federated identities to user-centric identities (Allen 2016). To understand the current problems of identity management, their origin and why blockchain technology might be the perfect infrastructure for decentralized identity solutions, a brief historic review of digital identity evolution is provided in the following.

In the early years of the internet, identity was provided by centralized authorities, which certified and authenticated the validity of IP addresses (IANA; Internet Assigned Number Authority), domain names (ICANN; Internet Corporation for Assigned Names and Numbers) or digital certificates for commercial websites (CA; certification authorities) (Allen 2016). Such hierarchical organization of control is still part of the internet today, whereas certificates, domain names and service providers rent those to users. Federated identity-management accounts for the fact that individuals frequently move between services and service providers. A federated identity enables a user to store electronic identity attributes on multiple identity-management systems (Norlin & Durand 2002), for example, by Google to increase the usability and usage of their product and service portfolio. A category of federated identity management is the single-sign-on (SSO; Samar 1999), which enables users to sign up and log in with multiple organizations and service providers with the same credentials, namely a username and password. An increased usability and frictionless service provision improves user experience and behaviour but reintroduces the problem of a single point of failure, which leaves the user without any means of control or action. Federated identity systems reduce the burden of multiple fragmented identity solutions for users, but still build upon the centralization of control among these federated authorities. During the first decade of this century, several initiatives focused on creating models of identity, which put the users at the centre of control. The initial ideas for reorganizing control over personal data, decentralizing trust and facilitating the portability of such data across providers have never been met and solutions have not experienced widespread adoption. Rather than building upon these ideas, Facebook can be regarded as a step backwards. Facebook users do not have the choice among identity service providers but provide all data to Facebook itself. The company is in complete control of its users' data and accessing other websites and services using such Facebook identity creates the risk of losing multiple identities at once, if Facebook fails to secure data or revokes access (Allen 2016).

For individuals, being in control of their personal data is referred to as "sovereignty", the concluding concept is referred to as self-sovereign identity. It could be regarded as the next evolutionary step of digital identity following the user-centric approach. There is no consensus about what exactly defines self-sovereign identity, but it must include the user being central to the administration of its identity in an autonomous way (Allen 2016). The term and idea of self-sovereign identities has been shaped during the last decade and before blockchain technology was identified and terminologically decoupled from Bitcoin. Building upon the "laws of identity" (Cameron 2005), the respect network policy (RNC) and the W2C verifiable claims task force (W3C), Allen identifies ten principles that must be inherent for self-sovereign identities to fulfil their promises (see Table 4.3).

In fact, such principles have been partly recognized by politicians internationally. The General Data Protection Regulation (GDPR) of the European Union does recognize and establish users' rights towards companies which seize personal data, to allow for their portability from one provider to another. In addition, the "right to be forgotten", meaning a person's right to have personal data deleted, has been manifested in the EU regulation. However, while the GDPR is a unique framework for empowering users over their data, it is still far from empowering individuals to control their data autonomously in the sense of a self-sovereign identity.

Blockchain technology has been identified to provide the infrastructure for building identity-management applications, which are decentralized

Table 4.3 Principles for self-sovereign identity

Principle	Description
Existence	Any self-sovereign identity cannot exist wholly in digital form – users must have an independent existence. A self-sovereign identity simply makes public and accessible some limited aspects of the independent individual that already exists.
Control	Subject to well-understood and secure algorithms that ensure the continued validity of an identity and its claims, the user is the ultimate authority on their identity. That is, users must control their identities. They should always be able to refer to it, update it, or even hide it. Other users may make claims about a user, which the user cannot control, but they should not be central to the identity itself.
Access	Users must have access to their own data. A user must always be able to easily retrieve all the claims and other data within their identity. This does not mean that a user can necessarily modify all the claims associated with their identity, but it does mean they should be aware of them.
Transparency	The systems used to administer and operate a network of identities must be open, both in how they function and in how they are managed and updated. The algorithms should be free, open-source, well-known, and as independent as possible of any particular architecture.
Persistence	Preferably, identities should last forever, or at least for as long as the user wishes. Although private keys might need to be rotated and data might need to be changed, the identity remains. This must not contradict a "right to be forgotten"; a user should be able to dispose of an identity if they wish and claims should be modified or removed as appropriate over time.
Portability	Information and services about identity must be transportable. Identities must not be held by a singular third-party entity, even if it is a trusted entity that is expected to work in the best interest of the user. Transportable identities ensure that the user remains in control of their identity and can also improve an identity's persistence over time.

(Continued)

Table 4.3 *(Continued)*

Principle	Description
Interoperability	Identities are of little value if they only work in limited niches. The goal of a twenty-first-century digital-identity system is to make identity information widely available, crossing international boundaries to create global identities, without losing user control.
Consent	Users must agree to the use of their identity. Any identity system is built around sharing that identity and its claims, and an interoperable system increases the amount of sharing that occurs. Such sharing of data must only occur with the consent of the user.
Minimalization	Disclosure of claims must be minimized. When data is disclosed, that disclosure should involve the minimum amount of data necessary to accomplish the regarded task. For example, if only a minimum age is called for, then the exact age should not be disclosed. This principle can be supported with selective disclosure, range proofs, and other zero-knowledge techniques.
Protection	The rights of users must be protected. When there is a conflict between the needs of the identity network and the rights of individual users, then the network should prioritize the freedoms and rights of the individuals over the needs of the network. To ensure this, identity authentication must occur through independent algorithms that are censorship-resistant and force-resilient and that are run in a decentralized manner.

Source: adapted from Allen (2016).

to allow individuals (and other entities) to exchange attributes and verify claims without depending on a central authority. Public blockchain systems could be employed as an access-control infrastructure as well as a tamper-proof storage for hashes, which serve as pointers for the actual data. The actual data is not stored on the respective blockchain but on a decentralized storage network, which parcels the data in an encrypted form onto several nodes, or on a third-party provider's cloud.

Figure 4.3 presents a proposed system by Zyskind and Nathan (2015) including four involved entities: user, service provider, nodes of the respective blockchain system and a storage facilitation, the latter of which could be run by another network of incentivized nodes. The user is interested in using applications, which are provided by service providers. The service providers are processing data for operational and business-related reasons, so as to personalize their services and offerings. The nodes are incentivized to maintain the blockchain in the way described in Chapter 2 on hash algorithms.

The proposed system in Figure 4.3 requires two new types of transactions: a transaction specified for access-control management (T access) and a transaction specifically for data storage and retrieval (T data). For each service that a user signs up for, a new digital identity is generated in the form of a public key using a transaction type "T access". The public key is shared with the service provider along with the permission to access data as has been pre-defined. Such permission is granted technically, which means that it can be revoked at any time by the user. The data that permission has been granted for by the user stems from either

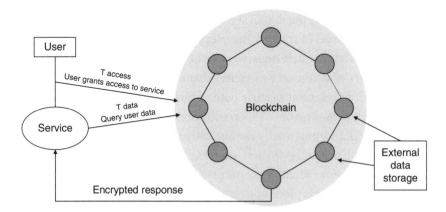

Figure 4.3 Visualization of the relationships in blockchain-based identity management

Source: adapted from Zyskind & Nathan (2015).

139

existing data being uploaded or data generated in the course of using the regarded application, such as geo-location data. Such generated data is encrypted by a shared encryption key and sent to the blockchain using a T-data transaction. The blockchain does not store this data but routes it to the data storage network and keeps only a hash of the data.

The principle is installed that a service querying that data needs to have an access permission which is being checked automatically. Moreover, querying data from the data storage using T data in the blockchain system requires an associated digital signature. This signature was mathematically generated when the identity was created and, in this example, the only valid ones are those of the user and the service. A foreign service could potentially request access to that data. Through the digital signature of this provider, the user can verify that the service provider is the one it pretends to be, and eventually grant access. Imagine a service provider wants to make use of personal data to personalize offerings or train an algorithm and is willing to pay for the data access. Following this, the setting is prone for a data economy in which users are in control of their data and those companies who want to utilize it, pay for it accordingly.

However, there is a need for trusted entities to authenticate, verify and digitally sign information which is technically associated with an identity. That is, verifying the digital signature of a service provider would require a certain level of trust by the user towards a registry, where public keys are registered. Such registries could potentially be maintained by the chambers of commerce of central banks (Baars 2016). Personal information of users, such as their date of birth, could be digitally signed as true by state authorities. This reintroduces the necessity of trust towards central and potentially manipulative entities, but as it has been outlined in the principles for self-sovereign identities, applications must be designed to make identity claims persistent. That is, once information has been verified, this piece of data (as part of the identity) exists until a user revokes it.

The design of public blockchains is qualified for access-control management through its implemented public-key infrastructure. The blockchain thereby acts as a container for metadata of user information, which can selectively be forwarded by users towards service providers. The scope for self-sovereign identity applications must be to allow users for selectively sharing aspects of their identity and maintain an auditable trail of which data was shared, with whom and when. Moreover, proving characteristics of one's identity without revealing actual information, such as proving to a service provider that one is older than 18 without disclosing the actual age, is a feasible feature. There are more technical approaches to utilizing blockchain technology for identity management in the like of self-sovereign identities – numerous projects are exploring and developing solutions.

Concepts and applications of digital identities in connection with blockchain technology are currently being researched extensively and are already being offered in the form of dapps: a signal that the potential has been recognized. It remains to be seen, however, to what extent such systems can establish and assert themselves. An essential point for the widespread use of such systems is that users become aware of the value of their data and recognize the importance of its security, which has yet to become the case. Governments may need to act on behalf of their citizens and legislate accordingly. The GDPR in the EU is an initial step but more research and development is necessary from public and private sectors to improve and secure personal data sharing and identity management in an increasingly digitized society.

4.4 CAPITAL MARKETS AND SECURITY SERVICES

Clearing and settlement

Security markets suffer from an inefficiency between the occurrence of trades and the actual time it takes to process the deals. The consolidation of positions often occurs once a day, while traders may only hold a security for minutes or split-seconds. This leads to so-called "netting" or "offsetting", situations where it remains unclear which entity owned a specific security at a specific point in time. Yet, obligations and rights, like dividend claims, voting rights and tax obligations are tied to specific times. The current legal system of various jurisdictions allows multiple ownership of securities at the same time, which represents a problem for days where dividends are paid out or where tax obligations are recorded. The level of uncertainty in the market is open to abuse by bad actors through so-called dividend stripping, a process that exploits legal loopholes.

One major innovation of the internet is that it enables the duplication of digital content and the sharing of this information with others. Original data remains with the first owner and digital copies are broadcasted. For non-sensitive information, like email communications, this system is fully sufficient. Yet, actual value that needs to be tied to a single owner and should not be duplicated, like money or security ownership, is not suitable for such a system. Therefore, centralized entities, like Clearstream for securities, act as trusted middlemen that maintain a central register to process and settle transactions. As discussed already, intermediaries face transaction costs (Clearstream services need to be paid for) or incentives for manipulation and fraud. The system represents a single point of failure that, if successfully attacked, can result in system-critical consequences.

The internet protocol suite (TCP/IP) enables information transfer via the web and blockchain protocols enable value transfer via the web. Blockchain technology comes with underlying consensus mechanisms that were explained earlier in this book. To this date, various different blockchain protocols have been introduced and there is no single commonly accepted protocol like TCP/IP. Similarly, internet protocols competed for dominance at the emergence of the web, so it is likely that blockchain standards will emerge in the future. Yet, it remains unclear if there will be one single blockchain protocol; it is more probable that there will be multiple specialized protocols – one being specialized for asset transfers and documentation for example. The European Central Bank (2016) highlighted clearing and settlement of securities as a specifically promising area of blockchain technology already in 2016.

A permissioned system that is at least to some extent shared with all network participants likely represents the best fit for a blockchain-based

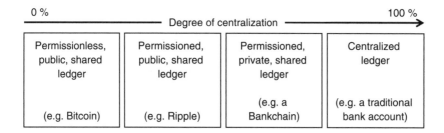

Figure 4.4 Blockchain fit for clearing and settlement of securities

system for clearing and settlement. Various protocol specifications in regard to existing legal structures, access constraints, consensus mechanisms or scalability need to be ensured. Bearing in mind these specifications, the fit of existing blockchains could be evaluated or new blockchain infrastructure could be designed.

The following example of blockchain-based determination of voting rights demonstrates the potential of blockchain technology in the field of securities trading. In securities markets, it is common practice that shareholders transfer their voting rights to third parties, like their bank. By introducing a blockchain-based system, processes can be made cheaper and more efficient, as the full ownership records are (semi-) transparently recorded and handled.

The process is made up of the following essential steps:

1. The shares of a company are tokenized. This can be a specific fraction of them or all existing shares. Each share is represented by a digital token on the blockchain.
2. Tokenized securities can be traded across the network. Transactions are immediately settled and recorded on the blockchain that contains the full record of past and current share ownership. There is no limit to the number of different stocks, as the blockchain can handle multiple tokens by specifically marking them. The decentralized and distributed architecture allows for a comprehensive and up-to-date picture of who owns how many shares. Yet, access to this information can be custom-built. For

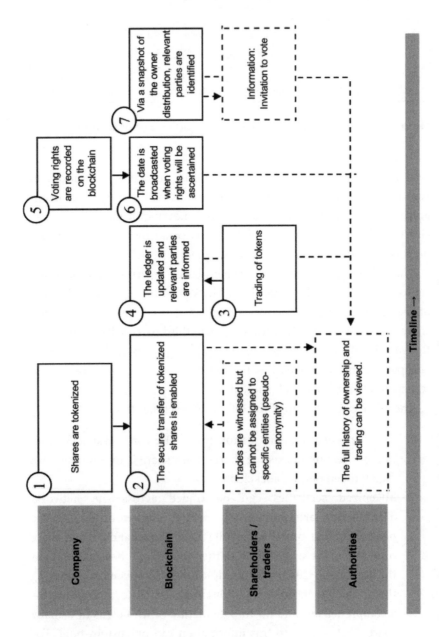

Figure 4.5 Blockchain-based determination of voting rights

example, the blockchain can allow specific users, like the company itself and the authorities, full access to all records, while other users are only able to monitor the network without gaining full-level insights. Shareholders and traders can witness all transactions but cannot assign them to the individual actors.

3. The process of securities trading can be built in two possible variants. First, tokens fully replace shares so there are no more paper-based shares that co-exist. In this variant, all trading and settlement processes would be shifted to the blockchain. The blockchain will then represent a decentralized intermediary that enables trading and monitoring. Second, tokens only represent shares: so-called digital twins. In this case, the blockchain system only represents a monitoring system, as effective trades are still done off-chain.

4. Once a transaction is successfully settled, and consequently the ownership structure of the company changed, records are updated on the blockchain and respective rights and obligations are automatically changed.

5. By sending a specific request to the blockchain, the company can initiate the distribution of voting rights for specific purposes, like an upcoming shareholder meeting.

6. The information about the specific timeframe in which possession of the stock grants access to voting rights is propagated in the blockchain network (and the public). Anyone is now able to trade shares in order to gain access to voting rights.

7. At the announced time, a so-called snapshot (one-time record) of the blockchain is made and shareholders that are entitled to voting receive their invitation.

Blockchain can even be applied one step further. The voting procedure itself can be conducted via the blockchain by signing digital messages or by transferring custom tokens that are solely created for this purpose. Similar techniques are already applied by exchanges in the blockchain ecosystem. For example, the cryptocurrency exchange Ethfinex distributed "Ethfinex Voting Tokens" in anticipation of specific decisions to holders of a specific asset. Owners of the voting tokens can then participate in votes on future processes. One innovative feature of the blockchain is that anything can be tokenized and traded on secondary markets. Ethfinex allows for trading of voting tokens on their platform. This way, voting rights and asset ownership rights can be split, enabling owners to 1) vote themselves, 2) transfer their vote or 3) sell their voting right. This process can easily be applied to traditional capital markets. The validity of votes can immediately be ensured. In theory, the blockchain can act in the background, as a basis for processes. No existing processes need to be fundamentally changed – just the underlying technology.

In this example, benefits arise from the greater ease of identifying and notifying holders of a company's share at a relevant point in time. In today's clearing and settlement infrastructure, by contrast, voting processes are costly and exposed to fraud. Transaction-processing can consume several days, resulting in difficulties to identify the exact distribution of the shareholdings and thus obscuring voting rights.

In addition to that, a decentralized database like the one of a blockchain provides the highest level of transparency for regulatory supervision. Costs of harmonization between databases can be reduced and potentially critical processes like asset rehypothecation can be monitored in real time, reducing the risk of a future financial crisis.

Initial coin offerings

Initial coin offerings (ICOs) (Ante *et al.* 2018) are a phenomenon that emerged in 2013. Essentially, projects sell digital tokens to contributors across the globe that represent a future function or use in the project's business. For instance, tokens can represent a complementary currency or a software licence. The ICO market experienced a rapid growth between 2015 and 2018 and is currently merging with traditional security and crowdfunding markets. ICOs present risky investment opportunities but paved the way for worldwide access and profit from companies' growth.

Initial coin offerings or token sales are a new form of corporate financing through the issuance of blockchain-based tokens. In contrast to traditional methods of corporate financing, companies may not sell equity in a token sale, but rather a token that represents some form of value for investors. In principle, a token sale can be defined in such a way that a project generates a digital token and sells part of it to token-buyers who expect the price of the token to rise or who want to use the issued token (for instance as a voucher or software licence). In contrast to an initial public offering (IPO), a token sale does not have a secondary market when the tokens are issued, since a listing on so-called crypto exchanges only takes place after the token sale has been completed. The token sale is therefore primarily oriented towards the output of the tokens.[1]

In principle, the concept of ICOs can be classified as a special form of crowdfunding or crowd-financing. Through the use of blockchain technology, this special form of financing can enable various characteristics that other or classic methods cannot. These include, for example, fast access to liquidity, since tokens can be traded comparatively quickly on secondary markets, or the above-mentioned variety of different characteristics that a sold token can possess. This can lead to completely new transactions, such as the tokenization of small quantities of an asset. In addition to classic tradable assets such as corporate investments, this can also involve real estate, ships, art or intangible assets.

A token sale can generally be viewed from three different perspectives: (1) token-buyer/participant who wants to buy a token; (2) society as a whole; and (3) the project that wants to collect funds (enterprise). The token-buyers identify and analyze a project with regard to its potential added value. The way the token-buyers identify with the project plays an important role. Either as a supporter of a new technology, for which they are enthusiastic, and thus have a long-term holding plan, or as passive investors, who are primarily interested in the return on investment (ROI). Investors can be users at the same time.

---

1. So-called initial exchange offerings (IEOs) represents ICOs that are directly conducted by secondary markets. In this case, token do have a secondary market directly after all tokens have been sold or the offering period has expired.

Various interests can be identified from the perspective of society as a whole. The overall economic interest in financing innovative companies has to be weighed against the risk of abuse and the overreach of consumers. The applicability of capital market law should also be seen in this context. From the point of view of the company, the question arises as to how far a token sale can be the appropriate method to finance a company or an idea. Sooner or later, a company will be faced with the question of how exactly it can and should be financed. External resources in the form of investments are often used for this purpose. At the present time, only a small number of global companies have the opportunity to finance themselves via the capital market. The concept of tokenizing and trading tokens can change this in a positive way. In principle, any company can digitize business shares relatively simply using blockchain technology. These can initially be sold on primary markets via ICO, in the case of securities, so-called security-token offerings (STOs) (Ante & Fiedler 2019) or simply digitized so that companies can offer these shares on secondary markets.

While a classic bank loan is often not accessible to small- and medium-sized enterprises (SMEs), the only way for start-ups to finance themselves is through a business angel or to obtain venture capital, in addition to family and friends. Business angels can be described as private and wealthy individuals who usually do not have family relationships with an entrepreneur, and who bring money, experience and their network into a company (Deakins & Freel 2003). Classic venture capital is another method by which companies can finance themselves. Venture capital companies often operate as funds that bundle the capital of various investors into start-ups. Compared to business angels, venture capital companies often invest in start-ups at a later stage when their investment volume exceeds 3–4 million dollars. Nevertheless, there are venture capital companies that also invest in companies at very early stages in order to prepare a company for later financing rounds or sales. Research shows that start-ups tend to sell a higher proportion of shares to venture capital companies than business angels (Kim & Wagman 2016).

Crowdfunding has established itself as a further source of financing in recent years, although it can be differentiated into four different forms: (1) donation-based, without consideration; (2) performance-based, with non-financial consideration in the form of services or items; (3) credit-based, with financial compensation such as interest; or (4) equity-based, with financial consideration in the form of equity or dividends.

The token sale model is a new form of crowdfunding or crowd-investing that can be roughly classified into one of these four forms of crowdfunding, depending on its design. Nevertheless, there are essential differences, which lie in the decentralization of the blockchain technology as well as in the free design of the functionality of the token through smart contracts. It should also be borne in mind that there are no liquid secondary markets in classical crowdfunding. In contrast, tokens can often be transferred relatively easily to special trading platforms, thus creating a market. Obviously, this is the biggest incentive for most participants in token sales. In classical financing via a bank or venture capital, the added value is limited to allocated funds and possibly still under the guidance or mediation of contacts. A further advantage of token sales is that investors have financial motives on the one hand, but on the other hand believe in the product themselves or want to use it. In this way, corporate financing can be combined directly with marketing. This can result in a cascade that financial success of the token results in a strong network of supporters and users. The simple cross-border use of blockchain assets offers a considerable advantage over traditional financing options. Even small projects are able to sell their tokens to investors worldwide and thus build up a network.

At the beginning of every token sale there is an idea, the implementation of which requires financial means or contributors. As soon as a token sale has been selected as a suitable instrument by a project, a preparatory process follows, which extends to the public announcement. In this process, the project evaluates the jurisdiction in which a company that may yet be founded will be located and takes care of legal formalities. At the same time, the content is prepared by selecting the token economy, technical and business information (including whitepapers), the website and human resources. It must be identified how exactly a token can have a utility value, but at the same time should generate the interest of participants in the token sale. The value of the company can be in the network itself (e.g. Ethereum) or (partly) in the company itself.

In addition, the technical feasibility of the project must be clarified. Which parts of the business model can be implemented within the decentralized approach of the blockchain, which parts should remain centralized? What is the financing need and how fast will the attraction of new human capital or services conclude? Based on these questions and processes, a company can draw the necessary information to assess when it needs which financial resources to implement the project. This includes the preparation and the process of the token sale, but also the actual development after the process. The great financial success of some token sale projects, such as Ethereum, has resulted in the market for ICOs experiencing extreme growth, and afterwards, a steep decline. From this process only selected projects will successfully emerge, and a multitude of projects will disappear, similar to the appearance of the first internet companies.

With the great success of Ethereum (Buterin 2014b) and smart contracts, the general token sale process has clearly changed. Between 2013 and 2015, a normal token sale was a token-buyer sending Bitcoin or another currency to a project-specific address and then (manually) issuing tokens to token-buyers at a certain point in time. Nowadays, token sales usually run via smart contracts – deterministic logic on the blockchain in the form of computer code. A project creates a smart contract that says, for example, "For each ETH that arrives, send back X of the new token. As soon as quantity Y ETH has been received, refuse any further deposits." This allows the token sale process to be fully automated: token-buyers receive their tokens immediately and these can be traded on crypto exchanges after a completed listing process.

In a "classic" token sale, in which a token is sold with a use (so-called "utility token"), a corresponding token economy must be created in which the use of the token for token-buyers and future users becomes obvious.

The start-up Golem (2016) is working on making computing capacities accessible de-centrally via a blockchain-based network. In principle, every user of the system should become able to make the superfluous computing capacities of a computer available to other users worldwide via Golem. To this end, the company sold the Golem Network Token (GNT) in a token sale and financed itself through it. Due to the underlying characteristic that the purchase and sale of computing power can only be paid for with GNT, the benefit of the token is clear. Every user of the network needs GNT to participate. Since the token has a fixed quantity and no underlying inflation, a network effect is created with increasing demand and the price of the token rises. Token-buyers speculate that tokens will (1) have the promised utility in the future; and (2) also increase in price due to increasing users and demand.

If further mechanisms, such as burning (a process similar to the buybacks with shares), or lockups (which lead to deflation or shortage of such a "money supply") are introduced, potential returns for investors can be thought to be relatively simple. This, however, creates a problem or trade-off. In a model with high inflation, users of tokens are incentivized to spend and use them, while in a deflationary system there are incentives not to use or sell tokens, since an anticipated shortage in quantity can mean future profits. Against this background, an ICO's token model must, on the one hand, appeal to investors but, on the other, also guarantee the use of the tokens as soon as the product has been developed. The implementation of thousands of ICOs since 2013 has produced an abundance of economic models, the suitability of which have still to be proven in the future. Irrespective of this, there is great potential for society to learn lessons from these models.

4.5 SUPPLY CHAINS AND LOGISTICS

Logistics and supply-chain management are a sector for which blockchain technology could be very beneficial. Whenever a lot of data from various actors converge, potentials for efficiency gains can probably be identified by using the blockchain. This is especially the case with supply chains, as massive amounts of data are involved. Supply chains are directly connected to complex processes in the production or distribution of goods or data. Products can be digital or tangible and the supply chain of a product can only consist of two or more participating companies and service providers. In addition, various processes such as different geographical coordinates, payment transactions or transport conditions may exist. Traditional systems are sometimes problematic and expensive because they do not guarantee a high degree of transparency and yet are extremely complex. The industry faces challenges such as loss of information, delays in deliveries – the cause of which cannot be precisely identified – or problems relating to the origin of products (a very relevant example would be food-tracking).

Blockchain technology offers a way to record and store transactions and any form of digital process in a secure way. Additionally, processes can be automated via smart contracts. The biggest promise of the technology for supply chains is the creation of transparency. Every network participant is able to access the same data, which results in a single truth that is shared across the network. A blockchain can be used for any (semi-)transparent transmission and management of data. This can include, for example, contracts, the status of transported goods or the status of payments. Four different aspects of blockchain technology are of specific interest for application in the supply-chain sector (Table 4.4).

In conventional systems, transaction-processing is either coordinated centrally by a party involved in the supply chain or secured by service providers. In each case, this presents a central point of failure, which can lead to problems such as technical failures or false incentives. Operators or service providers could be incentivized to present false information or to change data in central databases. By exchanging data P2P via a blockchain no intermediaries are involved and the decentralized database is automatically updated with every transaction. This means that it is always possible to determine clearly who did what and when.

It goes without saying that a fully automated supply-chain process is more cost-effective than one between a large number of companies

Table 4.4 Blockchain technological beneficial aspects for supply chains

Aspect	Description
Fast transaction settlement	• Transaction-processing happens directly between peers, eliminating intermediaries. • The shared database (blockchain) is automatically updated. • Transactions are simultaneously executed across involved parties.
Low cost	• Validating is achieved through computing power, representing a cost reduction compared to manpower. • Elimination of intermediaries. • No coordination work required.
Transparent and auditable	• Open-source technology. • Transactions are visible to all involved entities. • Transactions can be traced on the blockchain. • Accounts are pseudo-anonymous, and therefore identifiable.
Reliable	• No single point of failure. • Immutable and irrevocable transactions.
Pre-defined logic	• Via the use of smart contracts, processes can be automated.

that exchanges information manually and employs individuals for this purpose. In particular, the elimination of potential service providers can lead to considerable cost savings. However, care must be taken to develop a common solution that can respond to any updates or changes, that can guarantee the exchange of participants in the supply chain and that can be implemented comparatively quickly by new participants. Such a system only promises high added value, if all participants can participate. For this reason, standards and certifications are an important basis for cooperation in traditional industries. Such standards are still being developed for blockchain technology. An apt comparison could be the development of the application layer of the internet-protocol suite. It has taken some time to establish a standard that is widely used.

Transactions on public blockchain infrastructure are never completely free of cost, as there must be some incentive to secure transaction validity – it does not necessarily have to be a financial value and can also be a social incentive. It must also be clearly delineated how much information is to be written into the blockchain and when. If each process is to be immediately documented via a blockchain, this could potentially generate high costs or even system failures. Depending on the system, it can also take different lengths of time to successfully place a transaction in a block. The complete storage of all data in a decentralized network makes little sense. Intermediate solutions can be a suitable solution to take advantage of a decentralized network, while continuing to build on the efficiency of central server applications. Data can be logged centrally and anchored to the blockchain via hash (or Merkle trees) at regular intervals. This way, the proof of the data's accuracy is securely and transparently anchored in the blockchain but does not require fees for many transactions.

To date, companies commonly store their data locally and privately. Additionally, data is stored in different business units and processes. Frequently, no overall ledger exists that enables direct communication between companies and communication within the company may also be inefficient. Blockchain technology can offer a shared and secure database that enables various efficiencies and new business models. The level of privacy and access rights to data can be specially designed, resulting in a system that provides a secure infrastructure for companies that do not need to trust each other.

The transparency of blockchain is also helpful for participants in a supply chain. The degree of transparency between participants can be pre-defined so that there might be partial time-limitations and restrictions on read-and-write rights. Taking the idea a step further, a public blockchain infrastructure could be developed, on which special supply-chain protocols are anchored, to which companies can connect and disconnect. Thus, it is conceivable that companies conduct business with each other, connect with each other via the protocol and separate again after the conclusion of the business relationship. Should a new business relationship arise in the future, the companies could reconnect using the protocol. Historical data would still be available and the necessary effort for mutual coordination would be considerably reduced. In this respect, there is great potential for the development of supply-chain protocols on public blockchain infrastructure.

Iansiti and Lakhani (2017) propose four stages of transformation in the logistics sector with the adoption of blockchain technology (Table 4.5). Whether blockchain's penetration of the logistics sector really takes place in these steps is still unclear at this point. Nevertheless, it is clear that there is significant potential. If blockchain does develop in this space, the application of the technology will likely pass unnoticed as participants of a supply chain will use the blockchain in the background as well as common encryption technology.

In the following, a simplified example of shipping and trade finance will be used to show how blockchain technology could change parts of the industry and make it more efficient. This simplified example involves financial transactions and the transportation of goods. In addition, there is an abundance of different participants in the process.

Trade finance can be described as a process, in which an importer and an exporter mitigate the risks of trade via the use of a trusted intermediary. This intermediary provides assurance to sellers and certainty of contract enforcement to buyers. If an importer and an exporter, or respectively an applicant and a beneficiary, would like to conduct business together, a trade dilemma occurs. The two businesses might be located in different countries and can therefore not simultaneously exchange goods and payment. The level of trust is low, as the two businesses are unwilling to trust an unknown company in a foreign state. The shipment of goods might take a long time, which is why both businesses prefer different options of payment. Importers prefer to pay once they received the goods (open account) and exporters prefer to receive payment before the initiation of shipment (cash in advance). In order to mitigate risks both for importer and exporter, the letter of credit (LoC) is one of the most common services used to mitigate

Table 4.5 Stages of transformation for logistics

Transformation stage	Description
Single-use	• Tracking, tracing and monitoring individual transports. • Monitoring fleet and vehicle-activity history. • Growing number of blockchain start-ups and infrastructure platforms.
Localization	• Tracking of paperwork processing. • Information-sharing can be individually influenced by individuals/users. • No need for active participation/blockchain knowledge. • Enabling users to choose specific products or goods (like eco-friendly food).
Substitution	• Customers are able to access the desired information about products. • Fraud and counterfeit goods risks are reduced. • Paperless transactions. • Information of supply chains can be accessed by anyone. • Technologies like QR-codes, RFID, NFC-tags or Wi-Fi are used effectively. • The lifecycle of products can be monitored. • Internet of Things (IoT) is integrated into vehicle communication.
Transformation	• IoT becomes operable. • The exchange of goods and payments becomes simplified. • Transactions costs are reduced. • Centralized (governmental) institutions become less involved.

Source: adapted from Iansiti & Lakhani (2017).

risks to a certain extent. The lower the amount of trust, the more risk mitigation needs to be carried out. Banks offer their services to both importer and exporter to mitigate risks that occur from international trade (BCG 2018).

Figure 4.6 provides an overview of the international trade-finance ecosystem. It shows that banks play a central role in the trade-finance ecosystem, as they handle the transfer of documents, risk mitigation, financing and payment. The transfer of documents occupies a high level of complexity, as many different trade participants are involved.

Banks offer their services to both importer and exporter to mitigate risks that occur from international trade. For a fee, banks offer products such as LoCs, banker's acceptance, and guarantees, which transfer a share of the transactional risk from the client to the bank. As shown in Table 4.6, various pain points can be identified in the current state (World Economic Forum 2016).

The transfer and tracking of documents represent a complex area of trade finance. By using blockchain technology and smart contracts, this complexity can be reduced. As a decentralized secure ledger, all

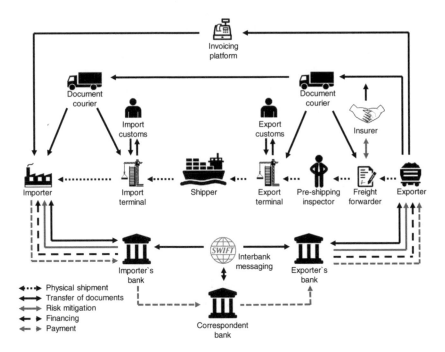

Figure 4.6 The international trade-finance ecosystem

Source: adapted from BCG (2018).

Table 4.6 Pain points in trade finance

Aspect	Description
Manual contract creation	Financial agreements are manually reviewed by the importer's bank after it receives the respective financial agreements and afterwards sends them to the correspondent bank.
Invoice factoring	Invoices are used to achieve financing in the short time for the exporter. This process leads to additional risks.
Delayed timeline	Intermediaries perform the checking of documents and goods multiple times, leading to a delayed timeline.
Manual AML review	AML checks are manually processed by the exporter's bank, upon receiving the financial statements from the importer's bank.
Multiple platforms	Counterparties use different and/or multiple platforms, leading to an increase of fraudulent risks.
Delayed payment	As various counterparties need to verify processes like the successful delivery of funds and documents prior to the disbursement of funds to the exporting bank, delayed payments occur.

documents can be uploaded to this ledger and be shared with others across the network. Smart contracts can be used to automatically check documents, notify involved parties of the upload and process modifications of documents.

Figure 4.7 shows how all participants of a trade ecosystem individually share documents and information using a blockchain infrastructure. This enables decentralized time-stamped file storage. The blockchain-based system of data management provides one possible solution how to develop and/or use a secure platform for trade-finance documentation. In this scenario, the blockchain is solely used as a non-financial platform to monitor the whole trade process. Any payments are handled off-chain but could possibly be carried out more quickly as the use of blockchain

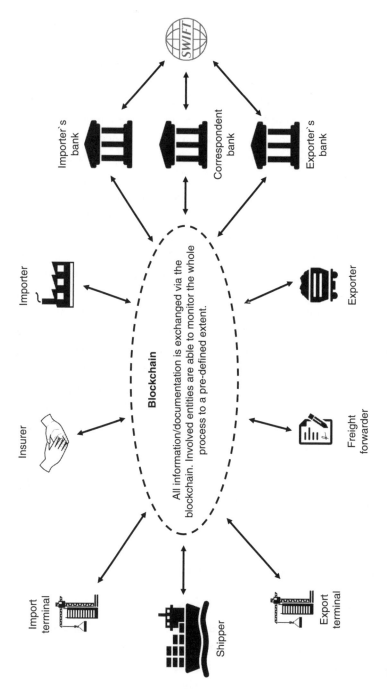

Blockchain

All information/documentation is exchanged via the blockchain. Involved entities are able to monitor the whole process to a pre-defined extent.

Figure 4.7 Blockchain document sharing in global trade finance

reduces the settlement time of a trade by eliminating back-office procedures, paper-based documents and manual processes. The blockchain
can only be used to monitor the trade process. Participants are able
to track the trade via the blockchain. Additionally, documents can be
shared via the distributed ledger. By uploading hashes of documents all
other involved players are able to check the authenticity of documents
on the blockchain. Therefore, no double-checking needs to be carried
out and individuals are automatically notified of any changes via smart
contract enforcement.

A LoC can be described as a bank's pledge to pay an exporter, once
certain documents are presented to the bank. An importer requests
this pledge from a bank after they have agreed a transaction with an
exporter. Based on the creditworthiness of this importer, some form of
collateral or cash deposit is possibly demanded prior to the creation of
the LoC. The importer has to inform the bank about the type of transaction, the documents needed to fulfil the LoC and of the amount of
the transaction. A LoC represents the promise of payout, once specified documents are handed in. This means in effect that a LoC is a
standalone contract dissociated from the original agreed terms of importer and exporter, which does not guarantee the transaction between
importer and exporter to be fulfilled. To be classified as a LoC, the contract must contain an expiration date, or a specified maturity and the
bank must collect a fee for issuing the LoC. A maximum quantity must
be specified and the payout of funds must only be tied to the presen-
tation of specified documents. Finally the importer who requested the
LoC must reimburse the bank of the exact value of payout the bank
pays to the exporter.

In general, the following steps belong to a LoC:

1. Importer and exporter conclude a contract (actually not part of
   the LoC).
2. The importer instructs their bank to issue a LoC.
3. The importer's bank initiates the process of a LoC and sends the
   respective invoice and documents to the exporter's bank.
4. The exporter's bank checks the LoC for formal issues and notifies
   the exporter upon successfully checking the LoC.

5. The exporter initiates the shipment of the goods. After shipping the documents, the exporter possesses all needed documents for the LoC and hands them over to their bank.
6. After, at minimum, a plausibility check is performed, the exporter's bank hands over the documents to the importer's bank.
7. The importer's bank checks the documents. On successful verification the bank notes an invoice of the documents and informs the importer of the successful check. The LoC is settled; in other words, the importer's bank orders payment based on the terms of the LoC or signals the verification that payment will be carried out at a given time.
8. The importer receives the goods (actually not part of the LoC).

A LoC is a highly complex product that requires the use of various intermediaries and a high degree of manual processing. Via a blockchain solution, pain points like manual contract creation, delays, manual checking and multiple reviews can be reduced or eliminated. In the following a blockchain-based smart LoC will be introduced, whose benefits contain real-time checking, automation, transparency, dis-intermediation and a reduced risk structure.

Figure 4.8 provides an overview of one possible approach to the application of a LoC in a blockchain ecosystem. The fundamental process consists of the following steps:

1. An applicant and a beneficiary conclude a contract with each other.
2. Jointly, they inform the blockchain (and smart contracts on the particular blockchain) of their conclusion of contract. As basis of this scenario, both their respective banks are already listed on the blockchain and can therefore automatically interact with relevant smart contracts.
3. Via a smart contract, the smart LoC is automatically generated, and the issuing bank is automatically informed of this contract generation. All information, like credit risk and underlying factors, is either automatically gathered by the smart contract or is added by the issuing bank via transaction.

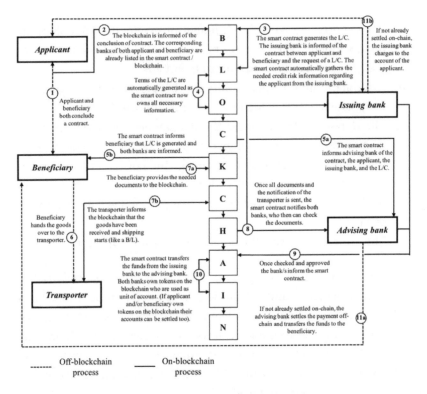

Figure 4.8 A blockchain-based letter of credit

4. On successful notification from the issuing bank, the LoC is automatically finalized and afterwards published on the blockchain.

5. Information of relevant parties: The smart LoC automatically informs the advising bank of the conclusion of contract, the identity of both contractors, the issuing bank and the terms of the smart LoC.

    a) The beneficiary is informed that the LoC is successfully generated and both relevant banks are informed of the procedure and the contract.

    b) The beneficiary hands over the goods to the exporter.

6. Provision of documentation:
   a) The beneficiary provides all required information and documents to the smart LoC via pre-defined input features of the smart contract.
   b) The transporter informs the blockchain via transaction that they received the goods and that the shipment is on its way. This information acts as a bill of lading (B/L) for the smart LoC.
7. Once the provision of documentation is completed, the smart LoC automatically informs both banks of this status of completion. Both banks are then able to check the documents. Possibly, the banks can agree on solely one bank being responsible for document verification.
8. Once the documentation is checked and approved by the banks the smart LoC is informed of this status.
9. The smart contract automatically transfers funds, in the form of tokens, from the issuing bank to the advising bank. Tokens can either be cryptocurrency like Bitcoin or specialized tokens that are solely used as unit of account between banks. Therefore, payments between banks can either be executed on the blockchain or solely be documented on the blockchain but being enforced off-chain.
10. Off-chain payments:
    a) Based on the assumption that both applicant and beneficiary do not use cryptocurrency as means of payment, the advising bank settles the smart LoC by transferring the respective funds to the beneficiary.
    b) The issuing bank charges the account of the applicant based on the terms of the smart LoC.

In summary, it can be seen that a blockchain-based smart LoC offers various benefits to the ecosystem of trade finance. In order to achieve these benefits, various critical conditions have to be met. Regulatory guidelines regarding procedures for LoCs and B/Ls have to be rewritten to enable real-time monitoring and/or transparency of trade processes on a blockchain. Another issue for the adoption of blockchain technology is the interoperability with various legacy platforms. As smart contracts should contain details of financing agreements, the interoperability of a blockchain must be provided.

As in many other cases in the area of supply chain and logistics, the success of such a system depends on the will of the participants. The biggest obstacles of wider blockchain adoption are network effects. Once all involved entities operate on-chain, a decentralized trade model could be implemented with relative ease. Given the fact that high fees from traditional LoCs are at risk, banks may not be willing to participate in such a model. In addition, such a system only offers real added value for participants in supply chains who do not trust each other. Trusted participants already pay in advance or via credit, so there might be no need for such a system. It seems unrealistic for participants who do not trust others to initiate such a system. State infrastructure is also only of limited help here, since participating companies do not usually come from the same jurisdictions. The most likely solution for the actual introduction of such a system is an open-source protocol, which has established itself as the market standard. Here, large and relevant companies in the respective areas must rely on the use of such systems, so that smaller companies follow suit.

While far-reaching models with many actors, as shown by the example of trade finance, possess enormous efficiency potentials for supply chains and logistics, application can be implemented much more quickly with only a few, possibly even only one participating entity. For example, the blockchain can be used to record and monitor internal supply-chain processes – even if the benefit of the blockchain itself is low in an individual company. Future developments will largely depend on the development of standards and regulations.

4.6 THE GAMBLING INDUSTRY

Gambling is, in its pure form, solely based on mathematics and associated both with positive emotions of winning and the negative emotions of (financial) loss. Lotteries or roulette are based on simple calculations. In roulette, for example, a gambler has a 1 in 37 chance of guessing a number correctly, but only of receiving a payout of 36 times that amount. This ensures that the operator always wins in the long run and there is no way to beat the system – except through fraud. With games that involve skill, such as poker, the odds are very different. The games that involve still based on simple probability calculations, but players play against other (human) players and not against the house. This means that above-average players can achieve positive returns – if they are better than their competitors and are also good enough to earn more than the provider charges in fees.

Due to the internet and the online gambling it facilitates, the boundaries between gaming and ordinary gambling are becoming increasingly blurred. On the one hand, games are offered in which it is unclear whether the game is still based on fair mathematics or whether specially designed algorithms merely suggest this. In addition, gambling elements are built into regular games (e.g. smartphone apps that use so-called loot boxes to monetize games via gambling mechanics). End users cannot judge whether they are playing against real people, whether they are "fed" by a mechanism or whether it is a simple game or gambling.

Blockchain technology has the potential to solve various problems associated with online gambling. However, like lots of innovative new technologies, it can also be used in detrimental ways. For this reason, gambling highlights the potential and the risks of blockchain. A potential vision of gambling via blockchain is the complete decentralization of all processes and an elimination of associated fees. Theoretically, a completely fair, transparent and secure gambling system can exist on the blockchain, which pays out any stakes deposited in full to players or winners of the games. However, such a system also contains various weak points. Ultimately, a precise analysis is needed to determine whether and how such innovations can bring benefits to society.

Blockchain can be applied to and have influence on gambling at three points: those of access, offer and value. These can be centralized or decentralized. Based on these three classifications, the following classifies existing gambling offerings on the basis of their characteristics (see Table 4.7 for their main forms). It should be noted that profit-making intentions in the form of fees are, in general, excluded from this analysis.

Table 4.7 Centralized and decentralized access, offer and value associated with gambling

Characteristic	Description
Access	How exactly can the gambling offer be accessed? Is it a classic website hosted by a gambling company? Is access offered as a decentralized code stored on the blockchain, which users have to execute themselves?
Offer	What is the gambling offer like? With a central offer, the logic can be either transparent or non-transparent (a black box). In the case of a decentralized offer, the logic of the gambling is anchored in the blockchain as a smart contract. Each person is able to call up the underlying code to make sure which logic the game is based on.
Value	How are stakes, winnings, losses, deposits and withdrawals processed? In a central model, values (which can be fiat currencies or cryptocurrencies) are sent to the provider, who then manages them centrally. In the case of a decentralized offer, values are sent, used and paid out directly via the blockchain using cryptocurrency. Players connect their account to the game and do not need an additional intermediary to process payments.

Table 4.8 Types of gambling and their degree of decentralization

Classification	Access		Offer		Value	
	C	D	C	D	C	D
1. Regular online gambling websites	X		X		X	
2. Regular online gambling sites that accept cryptocurrency as payment option	X		X		X	
3. Smart contract-based gambling offers through regular websites	X			X		X
4. Smart contract-based gambling offers that are built and hosted on decentralized infrastructure		X		X		X

C=centralized, D=decentralized

Online gambling websites: in classic online gambling, people visit a website, deposit money there, via bank transfer, and can use the offers on the website. As soon as a game is finished, the player can request a payout and the provider initiates a transfer of the remaining or won amount. In this case, all three categories are centralized and controlled by the provider or its service providers.

Regular online gambling sites that accept cryptocurrency as payment option: the basic transaction is the same as in classic online gambling, but the payment vehicle is crypto-based. Once cryptocurrency has been transferred, control is transferred to the provider in the same way.

Smart contract-based gambling offered through regular websites: in the third case, the gambling service will continue to be offered via a central website but will be provided via cryptocurrency and on the basis of smart contracts. Thus, offer and value are decentralized and transparent, only access to the offer remains centrally organized. In view of the fact that blockchain technology and the decentralized web are comparatively recent developments, user-friendliness remains an obstacle. Maintaining a centrally controlled access can make the site user-friendly. The only central points in the system are the hosting and building of the website, which remain potential problems for hacking of the central infrastructure or fraud attempts on the part of the provider.

Smart contract-based gambling offers that are built and hosted on decentralized infrastructure: in fully decentralized gambling, all processes involved, from access to offer to value, are offered de-centrally. There are no central points for attacks, no more deposits or withdrawals at providers in the conventional sense, as players either interact directly with the game itself and thus make payments themselves from their personal wallet or transactions are sent (partially) automatically directly to the addresses of users. This ensures monetary autonomy. Values will lie either with the game itself or with the user.

A game can run in a completely decentralized way and a provider or smart contract developer can continue to charge fees – in the case of a smart contract, they are charged transparently. A completely transparent blockchain gambling system can therefore continue to be very profitable for providers. Developments in the field of blockchain technology even make mechanisms conceivable in which decentralized gambling has payout quotas that are higher than the players' deposits. Thus, a lottery protocol can be conceived that lends players a stake during the course of the game through a different blockchain protocol (e.g. compound finance) and thus generates interest, which is then also paid out. With approaches like PoolTogether (pooltogether.us) similar initiatives already exist.

A completely decentralized gambling protocol can have advantages and/or disadvantages over conventional offers – depending on the point of view. It is often a trade-off between personal freedom and influence or protection by state institutions. Costs and benefits for society as a whole should be considered here. Even if full private autonomy might be a desirable condition, other issues such as player protection or the protection of minors presumably have a higher overall relevance. In Table 4.9, the main points are presented, listing the potential advantages and disadvantages.

Perhaps the biggest advantage or potential of blockchain-based gambling is the reduction of fees. A discontinuation or a considerable consolidation of gambling providers does not pose a considerable problem, as these are in most cases profit-driven companies that generate extremely high profits. At the same time, one must be aware of the fact that such an omission is extremely unlikely, since a decentralized protocol cannot carry out marketing and advertising in a comparable way. One solution could be the operation of such offers by state authorities. In this case, however, implementation seems equally unlikely against the background of incentive conflicts. In addition to protecting their citizens, states also have other objectives, such as maximizing their tax revenues. For this reason, it seems realistic that fair and transparent blockchain gambling will and can only cover a special niche of the market.

There is one important drawback that goes along with blockchain-based gambling. States and regulators are not in a position to prevent (possibly illegal) gambling or to enforce the protection of minors. This provides a platform for problematic, greedy or criminal machinations – history shows that technological innovation is often first exploited by criminals. For example, gambling allows a much higher degree of anonymity for players by means of cryptocurrency or decentralized gambling. In addition, cross-border transactions can be processed more

Table 4.9 Potential advantages and disadvantages of blockchain-based gambling

Topic	Potential advantages	Potential problems
Payments with cryptocurrency	• Fast deposits and withdrawals • Low-cost (cross-border) transactions • Independence of financial services like banks	• Irreversibility of transactions • Origin of funds unclear (e.g. money-laundering risks) • Loss due to hacks
Smart contracts	• Underlying calculations are transparent • Reduction of fraud • Automated market surveillance • Automated payouts	• Difficult to change or remove
Anonymity	• Higher level of personal privacy	• Problems identifying customers; KYC • Problem identifying minors, problem gamblers or criminals
Accessibility	• Ability to access from anywhere	• Inability to restrict or to terminate illegal gambling offers
Fee reduction	• Higher payout ratios for users and/or operators • Lower running costs for operators	• Existing operators go out of business
Decentralization via blockchain	• Immutable and secure processes • Dis-intermediation (no gambling operators)	• Lower efficiency

easily and quickly. From a regulator's point of view these are problems; from the user's point of view these can be advantages. The underlying property of the irreversibility of cryptocurrency transactions also means that unlawful or incorrect transactions cannot be reversed. Against the background of AML mechanisms, for example, this represents a difficulty that still needs resolution. The high degree of anonymity and the possibility of easily sending values across national borders make it difficult to find a solution. Time will tell the extent to which blockchain-based gambling can become a serious alternative to current online approaches.

While the blockchain as a technology can have a significant impact on gambling itself, the technology can also be used as a tool to make today's online gambling market more secure or to offer new types of services or gambling forms. For example, a customized currency or blockchain infrastructure can be used as a complementary ledger to process all gambling-related transactions. By making such a complementary currency the only permitted payment option for regulated gambling, it would be possible for a central (government) entity to precisely control and monitor which transactions take place in the gambling sector. Control of risky gambling transactions could in principle also be extended to other areas that are a high risk (e.g. chemicals or weapons) (Steinmetz & Fiedler 2019).

In the section on logistics, we explored how blockchain is also suitable for tracking processes. Gambling regulators could use the technology to set up a transparent solution for managing and controlling licences. Also, potential problems such as fraud or responsible-gambling programs could be tracked via the blockchain. Taxes could be paid immediately, which would make the system more efficient. All this can theoretically be based on the above model of cash-flow monitoring via blockchain.

The blockchain creates trust between entities that, in principle, do not or have no reason to trust each other. So, competitors in a market can use the same basis for information transfer without having to give each other complete data access. Gambling providers can use a blockchain-based infrastructure to exchange or log various processes with each other (or be prompted to do so by the government). Due to the immutability and (partial) transparency of the system, violations could be precisely identified at any time. If, for example, a compulsive gambler is blocked from participating in future games of chance, any further attempt logged by the player could be forwarded to other operators. In addition, in the event that this player does play successfully, it could be proven when and with which provider the game occurred. The player could assert their rights and the regulator could take appropriate action against the provider.

5

Conclusion: possible directions of blockchain

In this book, we have provided a comprehensive overview of the phenomenon of blockchain technology, its potential and its pitfalls. Blockchain technology holds significant disruptive potential for changing the way individuals, companies and authorities interact. Although Bitcoin was invented more than a decade ago, the innovative use of the technology that undergirds it has only recently begun and can still be regarded as being in its infancy. However, blockchain technology has to overcome some challenges and shortcomings in the near future for its full potential to be rolled out and for it to outperform existing centralized systems.

Other disruptive technologies, such as the internet, provide a paradigm for blockchain. While the basis of these technologies, the Arpanet, was already in operation in October 1969, it took many years until standards such as TCP/IP were established in 1981, and in 1989 the foundations of the World Wide Web were laid. The first browser was published in 1993 with Mosaic. From this point on, it was only through applications such as email that the internet actually began to be used extensively. Consequently, new, complex technologies that can change or displace the business models of established companies are not necessarily successful in the short term. We are at an early stage of research and experimentation with blockchain. While particular sectors can realize the benefits of the technology faster than others, various challenges still have to be overcome before standards are established and the technology can be applied safely and extensively.

The challenges for blockchain are technical, governmental and regulatory. The technical issues relate to the scalability of public blockchain systems. The price for the decentralization is that processing tasks need to be performed redundantly, as every validator node needs to process every transaction. The securitization of the system using complex consensus algorithms results in low transaction throughput, which makes them less competitive compared to conventional payment services like Visa. Moreover, block formation intervals are comparably long (13 seconds on average for Ethereum transactions, 10 minutes on average for Bitcoin transactions). These features are impractical and hinder its widespread adoption as a means of payment or for the use of time-critical applications. Potential solutions need to prove themselves to be as reliable and secure as the current design of Bitcoin's blockchain. Additionally, as the number of transactions increases, so does the data load of the whole blockchain. That is, the resources required to maintain a validator node, for example, bandwidth and storage capacities, increase over time, while they decrease validators' potential profits. This potentially results in an increasing centralization as fewer validators can afford these requirements in future.

In connection with the scalability issue, some of the consensus algorithms employed in blockchain systems are unsustainable in terms of their energy consumption, allow for destructive mining strategies (Eyal & Sirer 2018) and are prone to mining-pool centralization. Such tendencies of centralization are already happening today, as in the case of Bitcoin. An ongoing centralization in public blockchain systems is accompanied by the reduced resiliency of such systems, compromising both their usability and trustworthiness. The amount of energy dedicated to the Bitcoin system is immense and is rightfully subject to criticism. But, on the other hand, the energy adds up to a computational barrier against attacks, which is a crucial characteristic. While news of personal and sensitive data leaks from service providers is frequent, the Bitcoin blockchain has not experienced any such manipulation since its invention. More sustainable consensus algorithms are being developed and tested for reducing the computational and energy efforts of securing such systems and diminishing centralization tendencies in mining.

Highly decentralized blockchain systems are a difficult to govern. Their governance structures are not yet mature and are still in development. To survive, the systems have to adapt and keep abreast technical advances. Consequently, procedures and processes need to be tested, be reliable and be implemented so as to ensure the best structure for governance and standards. The vast number of new projects and ideas are overwhelming and potentially problematic. Some of these are simply replicas of successfully implemented blockchain code, rebranded to attract investors and projects to build applications. This can represent redundancy, but it can also facilitate the testing of different economic models. Calls for an increasing professionalization of the ecosystem surrounding blockchain technology development is symbolic. Research in the field of governance, consensus and incentive mechanisms, as well as for technical issues, will evolve and eventually contribute to overcoming the current limitations and problems of the technology. As history has shown, the most advanced and advantageous solutions survive, while inferior approaches fail.

The regulatory dimension of blockchain's challenges includes the extent to which governments realize the potentials of the technology and create regulations beneficial for innovation, such as the use and acceptance of cryptocurrencies and critical implementations in business settings. The temporary success of ICOs has been characterized by considerable legal uncertainty. A large number of companies have settled in countries that are innovation-friendly. The result being that in countries with comparatively strict regulation, innovative projects have migrated abroad, and this has by no means led to greater security for investors. The emerging ecosystem for security tokens offers significantly higher potential as tokens are sold as regulated financial instruments. This ensures that such offers are subject to capital market law and that the offer to investors of corresponding jurisdictions also has to comply with the corresponding regulations. It seems conceivable that this form of financing could lead to a transformation of capital markets and, in future, companies of all sizes will have the opportunity to finance themselves via the capital market.

One of the aims of this book is to make readers aware of the potential of blockchain technology by exploring specific applications. The six areas we have covered include applications that could already be implemented now (central-bank digital currency, ICOs), ideas that are further in to the future but offer great efficiency potentials (energy markets, identity) and applications whose implementation and/or application could have both socially desirable and undesirable effects (gambling). This selection of applications are only examples and blockchain-based applications are conceivable in virtually every industry.

Blockchain technology is not yet mature enough for a broad market. The ecosystem is testing various technological approaches, combinations with other technologies, fields of application and economic models. In the same way that the internet emerged, widespread use will depend on the establishment of standards and norms. It is unlikely that there will be only one blockchain standard; a variety of application case-specific standards and protocols is the most likely outcome. In this respect, it is quite possible that special standards will be established in the next few years, while others will take a long time to develop.

Blockchain technology might make future steps in combination with big data and artificial intelligence. While transaction data in blockchains themselves provide big data loads from which patterns are being extracted, blockchain's features might turn out to be advantageous for big data analytics as well. As with the example of digital identities, blockchains can serve as a querying and access permission-management system for vast data collections. Big-data collection and autonomous control over personal data is not a contradiction. It is perfectly possible that blockchain technology will enable the creation of a more transparent and fair data economy, by organizing data and processing payments in a trust-free manner.

Artificial intelligence might help blockchain technology evolve. in particular, artificial intelligence could be developed to independently and autonomously provide information to the blockchain through as oracles, which communicate with the blockchain to create signals for smart contracts. As today's oracle approaches reintroduce third parties on which peers interacting with a smart contract need to rely, artificial intelligence could be trained and train themselves to provide information independently.

In the foreseeable future, an ongoing professionalization of the industry will probably result in increasing automation through smart contracts and usage of dapps. An increasing sophistication of development tools, smart contract audits and functionality might attract new developers. More attention will undoubtedly be brought to trust-free and decentralized ecosystems, simply because the frequent coverage of leaked personal data will lead consumers to more secure and empowering applications of blockchains, eventually leading to a more widespread adoption.

Whether blockchain technology is able to unroll its full potential in the future has yet to be seen. Its promise for dis-intermediation, localization and the empowerment of the individual depends on many factors. But, the research and development of the technology is already paying off. Considering the potential societal changes that technology can bring, individuals, companies and governments should clearly focus on researching and testing the technology. Irrespective of whether blockchain as we now understand it will prevail, the idea of decentralizing processes has been implemented. Society will change accordingly, even if it is still unclear how much at the present time. We are at the beginning of a process that resourceful entities will prepare for and help build the next phase of digital interaction. We are on the doorstep to the internet of value.

References

Allen, C. 2016. "The path to self-sovereign identity"; http://www. lifewithalacrity.com/2016/04/the-path-to-self-soverereign-identity.html (accessed 13 April 2020).

Allen, D., C. Berg & M. Novak 2018. "Blockchain: an entangled political economy approach". *Journal of Public Finance and Public Choice* 33 (2): 105–25.

Alpár, G., J. Hoepman & J. Siljee 2011. "The identity crisis: security, privacy and usability issues in identity management". arXiv preprint arXiv:1101.0427.

Al-Saqaf, W. & N. Seidler 2017. "Blockchain technology for social impact: opportunities and challenges ahead". *Journal of Cyber Policy* 2 (3): 338–54.

Andoni, M. *et al.* 2019. "Blockchain technology in the energy sector: a systematic review of challenges and opportunities". *Renewable and Sustainable Energy Reviews* 100: 143–74.

Ante, L. & I. Fiedler 2019. "Cheap signals in security token offerings (STOs)"; https://dx.doi.org/10.2139/ssrn.3356303 (accessed 13 April 2020).

Ante, L., P. Sandner & I. Fiedler 2018. "Blockchain-based ICOs: pure hype or the dawn of a new era of startup financing?". *Journal of Risk and Financial Management* 11 (4).

Antonopoulos, A. 2015. *Mastering Bitcoin: Unlocking Digital Cryptocurrencies.* Sebastopol, CA: O'Reilly Media.

Antonopoulos, A. 2017. *Mastering Bitcoin: Programming the Open Blockchain.* Sebastopol, CA: O'Reilly Media.

Antonopoulos, A. & G. Wood 2018. *Mastering Ethereum: Implementing Digital Contracts.* Sebastopol, CA: O'Reilly Media.

Ba, S., J. Stallaert & A. Whinston 2001. "Research commentary: introducing a third dimension in information systems design – the case for incentive alignment". *Information Systems Research* 12 (3): 225–39.

Baars, D. 2016. Towards self-sovereign identity using blockchain technology. Unpublished Master's thesis, University of Twente; https://essay.utwente.nl/71274/1/Baars_MA_BMS.pdf (accessed 13 April 2020).

Baliga, A. 2017. "Understanding blockchain consensus models"; https://pdfs.semanticscholar.org/da8a/37b10bc1521a4d3de925d7ebc44bb606d740.pdf (accessed 13 April 2020).

Barrdear, J. & M. Kumhof 2016. "The macroeconomics of central bank issued digital currencies". Bank of England Staff Working Paper No. 605; https://www.bankofengland.co.uk/working-paper/2016/the-macroeconomics-of-central-bank-issued-digital-currencies (accessed 13 April 2020).

BCG 2018. "Embracing digital in trade finance"; https://www.swift.com/resource/boston-consulting-groups-paper-embracing-digital-trade-finance (accessed 17 August 2019).

Bech, M. & R. Garratt 2017. "Central bank cryptocurrencies". *BIS Quarterly Review*, September.

Beck, R., C. Müller-Bloch & J. King 2018. "Governance in the blockchain economy: a framework and research agenda". *Journal of the Association for Information Systems* 19 (10): 1020–34.

Berg, C., S. Davidson & J. Potts 2018. "Ledgers"; https://papers.ssrn.com/sol3/papers.cfm?abstract_id=3157421 (accessed 13 April 2020).

Bhargav-Spantzel, A., A. Squicciarini & E. Bertino 2006. "Establishing and protecting digital identity in federation systems". *Journal of Computer Security* 14 (3): 269–300.

Bitcoin Wiki 2020. "BIP purpose and guidelines"; https://github.com/bitcoin/bips/blob/master/bip-0001.mediawiki (accessed 13 April 2020).

Böhme, R. *et al.* 2015. "Bitcoin: economics, technology, and governance". *Journal of Economic Perspectives* 29 (2): 213–38.

Bonneau, J. *et al.* 2015. "Sok: research perspectives and challenges for bitcoin and cryptocurrencies". IEEE Symposium on Security and Privacy, 104–21. IEEE.

Brown, A. & G. Grant 2005. "Framing the frameworks: a review of IT governance research". *Communications of the Association for Information Systems* 15 (1).

Buchanan, J. & R. Faith 1987. "Secession and the limits of taxation: toward a theory of internal exit". *American Economic Review* 77 (5): 1023–31.

Buterin, V. 2014a. "On Stake". https://blog.ethereum.org/2014/07/05/stake/ (accessed 19 December 2019).

Buterin, V. 2014b. "Ethereum: a next-generation smart contract and decentralized application platform"; https://github.com/ethereum/wiki/wiki/%5BEnglish%5D-White-Paper (accessed 19 December 2019).

Cameron, K. 2005. "The laws of identity". Microsoft; https://docs.microsoft.com/en-us/previous-versions/dotnet/articles/ms996456(v=msdn.10)?redirectedfrom=MSDN (accessed 13 April 2020).

Carvalho, S. 2017. "Saudi working on digital currency for cross-border deals". Reuters; https://www.reuters.com/article/emirates-saudi-currency/update-1-uae-saudi-working-on-digital-currency-for-cross-border-deals-idUSL8N1OD2LP (accessed 13 April 2020).

Castro, M. & B. Liskov 1999. "Practical Byzantine fault tolerance". OSDI 99: 173–86; http://pmg.csail.mit.edu/papers/osdi99.pdf (accessed 13 April 2020).

Chao, Y. & L. Chen 2017. "China is developing its own digital currency". Bloomberg; https://www.bloomberg.com/news/articles/2017-02-23/pboc-is-going-digital-as-mobile-payments-boom-transforms-economy (accessed 13 April 2020).

Chaum, D. 1985. "Security without identification: transaction systems to make big brother obsolete". *Communications of the ACM* 28 (70): 1030–44.

Coase, R. 1937. "The nature of the firm". *Economica* 4 (16): 386–405.

Coeuré, B. & J. Loh 2018. "Central bank digital currencies". Committee on Payments and Market Infrastructures BIS Report; https://www.bis.org/cpmi/publ/d174.pdf (accessed 13 April 2020).

Davidson, S., P. De Filippi & J. Potts 2018. "Blockchains and the economic institutions of capitalism". *Journal of Institutional Economics* 14 (4): 639–58.

Deakins, D. & M. Freel 2003. *Entrepreneurship and Small Firms*. London: McGraw-Hill.

Deloitte 2019. "Continuous interconnected supply chain: using blockchain and internet-of-things in supply chain traceability"; https://www2.deloitte.com/content/dam/Deloitte/lu/Documents/technology/lu-blockchain-internet-things-supply-chain-traceability.pdf (accessed 13 April 2020).

Desai, V. 2017. "Counting the uncounted: 1.1 billion people without IDs". World Bank blog, 6 June; https://blogs.worldbank.org/ic4d/counting-invisible-11-billion-people-without-proof-legal-id (accessed 13 April 2020).

Dwork, C., N. Lynch & L. Stockmeyer 1988. "Consensus in the presence of partial synchrony". *Journal of the ACM* 35 (2): 288–323.

Engert, W. & B. Fung 2017. "Central bank digital currency: motivations and implications". Bank of Canada.

References

European Central Bank 2016. "Distributed ledger technology"; https://www.ecb. europa.eu/paym/pdf/infocus/20160422_infocus_dlt.pdf (accessed 13 April 2020).

Eyal, I. & E. Sirer 2018. "Majority is not enough: Bitcoin mining is vulnerable". *Communications of the ACM* 61 (7): 95–102.

Fama, E. & M. Jensen 1983. "Separation of ownership and control". *Journal of law and Economics* 26 (2): 301–25.

Fischer, M., N. Lynch & M. Paterson 1982. "Impossibility of distributed consensus with one faulty process". MIT Cambridge Lab for Computer Science, No. MIT/LCS/TR-282; https://groups.csail.mit.edu/tds/papers/Lynch/jacm85. pdf (accessed 13 April 2020).

Forbes 2018. "The future of social impact is … Blockchain"; https://www. forbes.com/sites/davidhessekiel/2018/04/03/the-future-of-social-impact-is-blockchain/#36718b1fc3fd (accessed 13 April 2020).

Frey, C. & M. Osborne 2016. "The future of employment: how susceptible are jobs to computerisation?". *Technological Forecasting and Social Change* 114: 254–80.

Friedman, M. 1969. *The Optimum Quantity of Money, and Other Essays.* New York: Aldine.

Fung, B. & H. Halaburda 2016. "Central bank digital currencies: a framework for assessing why and how". Available at SSRN: https://ssrn.com/abstract=2994052 (accessed 13 April 2020).

Garay, J., A. Kiayias & N. Leonardos 2015. "The bitcoin backbone protocol: analysis and applications". In *Annual International Conference on the Theory and Applications of Cryptographic Techniques,* 281–310. Berlin: Springer.

Garzik, J. 2015. "Public versus private blockchains"; http://bitfury.com/ content/5-white-papers-research/public-vs-private-pt1-1.pdf (accessed 13 April 2020).

Golem 2016. "White Paper". https://golem.network/crowdfunding/Golemwhite-paper.pdf (accessed 13 April 2020).

Griffin, Z. 2013. "Crowdfunding: fleecing the American masses". *Journal of Law, Technology & the Internet* 4 (2): 375–410.

Häring, N. 2017. "The E-Krona – Sweden's big digital currency idea"; https:// global.handelsblatt.com/finance/swedens-big-digital-currency-idea-846432 (accessed 13 April 2020).

Iansiti, M. & K. Lakhani 2017. "The truth about blockchain". *Harvard Business Review* 95 (1): 118–27.

iExec 2018. "White Paper"; https://iex.ec/wp-content/uploads/pdf/iExec-WPv3.0-English.pdf (accessed 13 April 2020).

Jensen, M. & W. Meckling 1976. "Theory of the firm: managerial behavior, agency costs and ownership structure". *Journal of Financial Economics* 3 (4): 305–60.

Kessler, G. 2016. "An overview of cryptography". https://www.garykessler.net/library/crypto.html (accessed 27 April 2020).

King, J. 1983. "Centralized versus decentralized computing: organizational considerations and management options". *ACM Computing Surveys* 15 (4): 319–49.

Kosba, A. *et al.* 2016. "Hawk: the blockchain model of cryptography and privacy – preserving smart contracts". In *2016 IEEE Symposium on Security and Privacy*, 839–58. IEEE.

Lamport, L., R. Shostak & M. Pease 1982. "The Byzantine generals problem". *ACM Transactions on Programming Languages and Systems* 4 (3): 382–401.

Liu, L. & N. Antonopoulos 2010. "From client–server to P2P networking". In *Handbook of Peer-to-Peer Networking*, 71–89. Boston, MA: Springer.

Manzato, D. & N. da Fonseca 2010. "Incentive mechanisms for cooperation in peer-to-peer networks". In X. Shen *et al.* (eds), *Handbook of Peer-to-Peer Networking*, 629–31. Berlin: Springer.

Mersch, Y. 2017. "Digital base money: an assessment from the ECB's perspective". Speech at the farewell ceremony for Pentti Hakkarainen, Deputy Governor of Suomen Pankki, Helsinki.

Meyer, D. 2017. "This country may launch its own virtual currency"; http://fortune.com/2017/08/22/estonia-estcoin-digital-currency/ (accessed 13 April 2020).

Moldoveanu, M. & R. Martin 2001. "Agency theory and the design of efficient governance mechanisms". Rotman School of Management, University of Toronto.

Nakamoto, S. 2008. "Bitcoin: a peer-to-peer electronic cash system"; https://bitcoin.org/bitcoin.pdf (accessed 13 April 2020).

Nicholson, J. 2017. "The library as a facilitator: how bitcoin and block chain technology can aid developing nations". *The Serials Librarian* 73 (3/4): 357–64.

Norlin, E. & A. Durand 2002. "Whitepaper on towards federated identity management". Ping Identity Corporation.

Obreiter, P. & J. Nimis 2003. "A taxonomy of incentive patterns – the design space of incentives for cooperation". In G. Moro, C. Sartori & M. Singh (eds), *Agents and Peer-to-Peer Computing*, 89–100. Berlin: Springer.

Ølnes, S. 2016. "Beyond bitcoin enabling smart government using blockchain technology". In *International Conference on Electronic Government*, 253–64. Cham: Springer.

O'Reilly, T. 2011. "Government as a platform". *Innovations: Technology, Governance, Globalization* 6 (1): 13–40.

Pan, J. *et al.* 2018. "Key enabling technologies for secure and scalable future Fog-IoT architecture: a survey". arXiv preprint arXiv:1806.06188.

PwC 2016. "Blockchain: an opportunity for energy producers and consumers?" https://www.pwc.com/gx/en/industries/assets/pwc-blockchain-opportunity-for-energy-producers-and-consumers.pdf (accessed 13 April 2020).

Reijers, W. & M. Coeckelbergh 2018. "The blockchain as a narrative technology: investigating the social ontology and normative configurations of cryptocurrencies". *Philosophy & Technology* 31: 103–30.

Reilly, M. 2017. "Japanese banks are planning to launch J-Coin, a digital currency meant to kill off cash"; https://www.technologyreview.com/2017/09/26/241990/japanese-banks-are-planning-to-launch-j-coin-a-digital-currency-meant-to-kill-off-cash/ (last accessed 27 April 2020).

Respect Network Corporation 2016. "The Respect Trust Framework"; https://oixnet.org/wp-content/uploads/2016/02/respect-trust-framework-v2-1.pdf (accessed 13 April 2020).

Salomaa, A. 2013. *Public-Key Cryptography*. Berlin: Springer.

Samar, V. 1999. "Single sign-on using cookies for web applications". In *Proceedings of IEEE Eight International Workshops on Enabling Technologies: Infrastructure for Collaborative Enterprises*, 158–63. IEEE.

Schneider, N. 2019. "Decentralization: an incomplete ambition". *Journal of Cultural Economy* 12 (4): 265–85.

Schwab, K. *et al.* 2011. *Personal Data: The Emergence of a New Asset Class*. Geneva: World Economic Forum.

Seddon, M. & M. Arnold 2018. "Putin considers 'cryptorouble' as Moscow seeks to evade sanctions". *Financial Times*.

SONM 2017. White Paper; https://whitepaper.io/document/326/sonm-whitepaper (accessed 13 April 2020).

Stallings, W. 2011. *A Handbook on Cryptography and Network Security: Principles and Practices*. Harlow: Pearson.

Steinmetz, F. 2018. "Using blockchain technology for the prevention of criminal activity". In K. McCarthy (ed.), *The Money Laundering Market: Regulating the Criminal Economy*, 199–222. Newcastle upon Tyne: Agenda Publishing.

Steinmetz, F. & I. Fiedler 2019. "A state-operated blockchain-based system for the transparent processing of online gambling payments in Germany". *Gaming Law Review* 23 (10): 715–25.

Szabo, N. 1997. "Formalizing and securing relationships on public networks". *First Monday* 2 (9); https://firstmonday.org/ojs/index.php/fm/article/view/548/469 (accessed 13 April 2020).

Tapscott, D. & A. Tapscott 2016. *Blockchain Revolution*. New York: Penguin.

Tepper, A. 2015. *The People's Money: Bitcoin*. Asia-Australia Technology.

Tschorsch, F. & B. Scheuermann 2016. "Bitcoin and beyond: a technical survey on decentralized digital currencies". *IEEE Communications Surveys & Tutorials* 18 (3): 2084–123.

W3C (World Wide Web Consortium) n.d. "Verifiable claims working group: frequently asked questions"; http://w3c.github.io/webpayments-ig/VCTF/charter/faq.html (accessed 13 April 2020).

Wagner, R. 2016. *Politics as a Peculiar Business: Insights From a Theory of Entangled Political Economy*. Cheltenham: Elgar.

Weill, P. & J. Ross 2004. *IT Governance: How Top Performers Manage IT Decision Rights for Superior Results*. Boston, MA: Harvard Business School Press.

White, M., J. Killmeyer & B. Chew 2017. "Will blockchain transform the public sector?"; https://www2.deloitte.com/insights/us/en/industry/public-sector/understanding-basics-of-blockchain-in-government.html (accessed 13 April 2020).

Wilkins, C. 2016. "Fintech and the financial ecosystem: evolution or revolution?"; http://www.bankofcanada.ca/wp-content/uploads/2016/06/remarks-170616.pdf (accessed 13 April 2020).

World Economic Forum 2016. "The future of financial infrastructure: an ambitious look at how blockchain can reshape financial services"; http://www3.weforum.org/docs/WEF_The_future_of_financial_infrastructure.pdf (accessed 13 April 2020).

Zhao, J., S. Fan & J. Yan 2016. "Overview of business innovations and research opportunities in blockchain and introduction to the special issue". *Financial Innovation* 2 (28).

Zheng, Z. *et al.* 2018. "Blockchain challenges and opportunities: a survey". *International Journal of Web and Grid Services* 14 (4): 352–75.

Zyskind, G. & O. Nathan 2015. "Decentralizing privacy: using blockchain to protect personal data". In *2015 IEEE Security and Privacy Workshops*, 180–84. IEEE; https://ieeexplore.ieee.org/stamp/stamp.jsp?tp=&arnumber=7163223 (accessed 13 April 2020).

Index